LIVE YOUR OPTIMAL LIFE

DR. DAVIA H. SHEPHERD AND
ELIZABETH B. HILL, MSW

with Shontelle Brewster, Robin H. Clare, LaQueshia Clemons,
Amber Dancy, Shannon Malkin Daniels, Annette Stahl Farha,
Mary Ann Francis, Ilja van de Griend, Robin Mayberry,
Jacquelyn Santiago Nazario, Mary Ann Pack, Gail Petrowsky,
Linda F. Piotrowski, Meghan Clemens Schelzi,
Noelymari Sanchez Velez, and Wendy Wolpert

ISBN Paperback: 978-1-954493-62-9

Published by Green Heart Living Press

Edited by Elizabeth B. Hill and Mary Ann Pack

Contents

INTRODUCTION

DR. DAVIA H. SHEPHERD

Thank you so much for picking up this Ladies' Power Lunch anthology. We are so grateful to share the outstanding stories of passionate women who have messages to share that are life-changing and inspirational.

I'm Davia Shepherd, and I host a women's group called Ladies' Power Lunch (LPL). Folx often ask me how LPL began. They ask, "How did you found LPL?" My response is always a little tongue-in-cheek, "I didn't found LPL! LPL found me!"

It all started when I left corporate life to join our private practice and had to learn about networking to grow my business. I was fortunate because I had the opportunity to meet a number of outstanding women in business in our community who embraced me immediately. One day, a few of us got together for lunch at a Ruby Tuesday on Route 6 in Bristol, Connecticut, and it was one of my best lunches on record to that date. All the women who were there were from different walks of life, but they all had one thing in common: they were committed to the idea of supporting each other so that we could all grow our businesses.

From that one lunch over ten years ago, we have grown into a group that not only spans the country but is multinational. The one thing that holds us all together is that we truly believe in the idea that when we support each other, everybody wins. We believe that there's no need to recreate the wheel. If there is something that a member is struggling with, we're pretty sure there's someone else in the group who has gone through this same thing, someone else who is willing to share her gifts and talents, and we all win, and we all grow together.

As I got to know our members more intimately through our LPL monthly networking meetings, our private members-only free Facebook group, and our LPL summits and retreats, what became very apparent to me is that these aren't just women in business. The membership of our group includes small business owners, larger business owners, solopreneurs, entrepreneurs, women in corporate life, women in non-profits, and retired women. As I got to know our members better through interacting with them more, I realized that these women are truly heart-centered and that they all have messages to share with the world to help make the world a better place.

The messages being shared out in the world at large aren't often those of love and light, and so I thought, *What would happen if we were able to share these positive, beautiful, life-changing messages from our LPL women with a wider audience? What would happen if we were able to share the stories and the life lessons of our members with the world?* Then perhaps folks who are losing sleep at night because they feel alone, who need these messages, maybe they could be helped. Maybe their lives could be changed, and maybe they could go on to help the people that they are meant to serve. I believe the world would be a better place.

So, Ladies' Power Lunch is definitely a place where women in business can come together and support each other to grow our businesses. It's also a place where women who are passionate about the things that they teach can use our platform—our Facebook group, LPL networking, the LPL TV show, LPL podcasts, summits, anthologies—to share their messages with about 20,000 to 50,000 of their ideal folks. And it's not through any kind of algorithm or any unnatural means that we are able to share in this exponential way—it's all through the power of collaboration and the power of women supporting each other in a very organized way.

I'm a very spiritually focused person and also a very practical person. If you had met me ten or so years ago, I would be asking you for double-blinded, placebo-controlled studies for just about everything. That's why it's important to me that as we share stories from our LPL members, we also offer our readers the opportunity to have their own transformation and to move a little closer to the ideal of living their optimal lives, knowing that there is never a stopping point and always more to aspire to.

This anthology features outstanding, vulnerably shared stories. In addition to the stories, at the end of each chapter is an opportunity for integration—an opportunity to answer some questions or do an exercise that will help solidify the lesson of the chapter. But wait, there is more! To launch this *Live Your Optimal Life* anthology, we hosted a summit featuring each author conducting a *Live Your Optimal Life* workshop. I invite you to go to growsmarternotharder.com/shop, and there, you will find bonus content as well as other LPL anthologies and summits.

One final thing: I invite you to join us. If you are a woman in business and the idea of being part of a loving, caring community of women who are committed to growing each other's businesses sounds amazing to you, then come join us. If you have a positive message to share with the world and you are passionate about what you do, then join us. It's easy, and it's free. Just go to growsmarternotharder.com/facebook. We can't wait to meet you and start supporting you!

Part I

Discovery

CHAPTER 1

BE THE EYE OF THE HURRICANE

DR. DAVIA H. SHEPHERD

Are you living your optimal life? Take a moment to close your eyes, think about living your optimal life (whatever optimal means for you), and just notice with no judgment what emotions are coming up for you.

Let me start by addressing the pink elephant in the room. Some of us might feel guilty for wanting the things we want, including wanting to have some aspect of our lives improved. We might struggle with feeling worthiness or not wanting to want "too much" when others have too little or something like that. Who has ever felt like that? I'm sure many of us have, me included. As with most things, I'm a work in progress and transforming out loud.

When we talk about living our optimal lives, let's preface this by saying that most of us reading this have pretty okay lives. We live with the privilege of having our basic needs met most of the time, so let's sit in a moment of gratitude for that. With a heart full of appreciation for all my gifts, I know both from my own experience, those shared with me by patients, as well as the women from the group that I host, Ladies' Power Lunch (LPL), that even though we have many things that are going well for us, many times there may be one or two things that may just feel stuck. We could be stuck for years, and this may even cause us pain and suffering.

What I know for sure is that if you are reading this, you are drawn to a life of purpose. I also know that living your life of purpose and sharing your message with the folx whose lives you are here to influence in a purely positive way is way easier when you are not in struggle, stress, and strain. Coming from the pure energy of your own optimal life energy allows you to resonate so much more clearly and easily with your people, increasing your impact and income in the way that you have the potential for.

I've always intellectually known that living my optimal life is possible for me. It's my aspiration, what I really want to do. The execution may sometimes be a bit wonky, but it's my goal, and it's more than that. I know that my true calling is to support the people who invite me to help them on their journey to living their optimal lives in whatever way that looks like for them.

The things that contribute to living an optimal life, or not, tend to, it seems, fall into one of six categories.

1. Relationships (romantic)
2. Relationships (family and friends)
3. Finances
4. Career, vocation, life's purpose
5. Health, wellbeing and wellness
6. Spirituality

Many of us may have four or five out of six things going well, but the one or two that aren't going well just seem to bring everything down.

So, in full transparency, I am not the poster child for living my optimal life. As a matter of fact, in many areas, I've been exactly the opposite of that. I work too long of hours, I overdo things, I leave myself off my own list, and I neglect my own self-care sometimes to the point of burnout. (It's happened. I have even developed a health issue as a result.) But what is important is that I know that I'm always a work in progress. I'm always striving to improve. I'm always focused on making sure that I'm doing things to get better and not beating myself up when I fall short of what I consider to be optimal. And when I look back at the experiences, I use them as moments of learning.

I'll share a story with you. Some of you might already know it; if this story is familiar to you, I invite you to sing along.

One of the six areas where folx focus on living their optimal lives is, of course, their health. As I started working in patient care, I realized that many people actually **expect** a decline in their health to be a part of getting older. They actually expect that after a certain point, it's all downhill. They think to themselves that there is no possibility of living their optimal life, at least as far as their health is concerned, once they get to a certain age or they get a certain diagnosis.

I remember having a conversation with a patient who had a diagnosis of diabetes. At first, it was devastating for her to get that diagnosis. She had to have her grieving process, but what stood out for me in such stark relief was that she was so committed to living her optimal life that she never let this diagnosis derail her, not fully. I'm not going to talk about the diet changes and exercise, supplements, and medication that helped her on her journey because that's not the point I'm trying to make here. What I want to share is that her attitude to this truly devastating diagnosis taught me a few things.

She shared with me that over the months prior to the diagnosis, she had been going through, in her words, "some things." She confided in me that as a result, her eating habits had been less than ideal, her exercise non-existent, and that would explain a bit why her diagnosis was as it was. She told me that, in a way, she was grateful for the diagnosis as it served as her wake-up call. It helped her to refocus on her health and wellness like it was her job. She even suggested that she was lucky to have this diagnosis as it made her realize how important her self-care and health care really is.

Her attitude, mindset, and commitment to living her optimal life, in spite of her circumstances, was a huge eye-opener for me. She went on to lose her unwanted pounds and got back into cycling, which was her favorite form of exercise and helped her commune with nature. She participated in a marathon, got a health coaching certification, and has gone on to help others who have issues with carbohydrate metabolism to change their mindset about their health, shed their unwanted pounds, and be healthier in mind, body, and spirit. She jokes that getting that diagnosis changed her life for the better.

Okay, I know what you're thinking. You're thinking that's a great story, Davia, and you're asking: *What does that have to do with me and me living my optimal life?* Well, I'm glad you asked.

I'm not saying that we don't have things going on in our lives that are difficult, challenging, and sometimes heartbreaking. As you will see from reading many of the other chapters in this anthology, life doesn't always go smoothly. One of my favorite mentors, Dr. Deepak Chopra, always talks about being the eye of the hurricane. He invites us to be able to *still*, and this is my interpretation: live your optimal life and *still* have that sense of joy and gratitude in spite of the things that may be showing up in our experience that might be less than ideal.

So, back to my patient: she got a diagnosis that would make every single one of us feel sad, uncertain, and maybe even a little bit terrified, and she spent some time sitting with it and experiencing emotion around it. At the end of the day, though, she didn't let it rob her of her joy, and I think that's the key takeaway. She also used the experience to grow and learn and help others, and so it really turned out to be a huge win for her.

How can you and me and everybody else who's tuning into this idea of living your optimal life lean closer to that idea of not allowing ourselves to be derailed by the circumstances of our lives? I find that when I focus on a few things, which I will share with you, it really helps me to stay on the path of living my optimal life and the joy that comes as a result of that.

It took me having my own health concerns to realize that this is true. The irony is not lost on me y'all. I work in healthcare, and my biggest struggle has been in the area of my own self-care, wellness, and health.

Some years ago, I had my baby and started in practice, all while the world was in an economic downturn. In order to grow my practice in an economically unstable world while taking care of my growing family, I was doing ***all the things.*** All the things except for taking care of myself in a kind and loving way. When I had pushed my body to its limit, some weird and wonderful symptoms started to show up. The short version of the long story: several physicians who couldn't figure out what was going on, and two unnecessary surgeries later, I finally was diagnosed with a rare, most likely stress-induced autoimmune illness. I wasn't taking care of myself, so my body forced me to stop and take care of myself.

Great news: Just like my patient that we chatted about earlier, my health is doing really well, and now I seem to attract a lot of my patients who struggle with autoimmune issues because I have had my own first-hand experience. I had a moment of despair with my health condition. But I never forgot the example of my amazing inspirational patient, and the bottom line is that I can live my optimal life as long as I'm able to focus on five super important things:

1. Picture

2. Practice

3. Process

4. Personal Care

5. People

I start with PICTURE.

As a kid, somehow, I may have gotten my wires crossed. I don't think this was the message my parents intended to send, but what I learned is that I should always sacrifice and that everyone's needs should come before mine. Somehow, I internalized that my needs don't matter. I embraced the idea that martyrdom is amazing. I spent a long time believing that I should always focus on everyone else's needs and that what I needed would automatically flow to me.

Now hear me out, dear one. Being kind to others is in my DNA. I get a rush, a true sense of happiness, when I'm able to do something nice for someone else. Talk about filling me with joy! That does it for me every single time. That being said, at no time growing up was I ever encouraged to really think about what I wanted, about what would make me happy, about what living my optimal life would look like. What about what makes me happy? What about what makes me tick? You'll understand why starting with "picture" is so important to me and why that also might be one of the more difficult pieces for me to implement in my own life when I am thinking about trying to live my optimal life.

So, what do I mean when I say "picture?" What I mean is take some time to get centered, perhaps take a few deep breaths, clear your mind, and then think about what it would look like for you if you were living your optimal life. What do you want? What aren't you allowing yourself to want but you secretly want anyway? What are your hopes, what are your dreams? When I'm in a workshop with patients or clients, we do an exercise called the **Optimal Life Star.** I'll include a version of it at the end of the chapter, but basically, what I'm inviting you to do now is to think about the six areas of your life and think about what it would really, really look like for you if you were living it optimally in the way that you want, the way that would make you drop to your knees in absolute and utter gratitude and joy because this is just exceeding all your amazing expectations?

What would it look like for you if you were living your optimal life in your relationships, both with your romantic relationships and your relationships with your friends and family? What would it look like for you if you were living your optimal life as far as your health, wellness, and well-being are concerned? What would it look like if you were living your optimal life as far as the decisions that you have to make about finances? What would your life look like if you were able to make choices based on desire and not on the price tag? What about work, your career, your vocation, your life purpose? What would you get up and do every single day with joy in your heart and no resentment whatsoever if you were living your optimal purpose? And what would the remuneration for that look like?

We're talking optimal life here, folx; there are no limits! No one is censoring this! I get to choose. You get to choose. Think about and feel into—what would it look like, what would it feel like, what would it smell and taste like, what would it touch like if you were able to have the sort of spiritual life that is optimal for you?

There's a saying, *"You have to see it to be it,"* and that's why I start with "picture."

The next area of focus for me is PROCESS.

I had the opportunity to explore a number of processes that support living an optimal life. What works well for you is going to be different from what works for someone else, but I'll share a few of the ones that work well for me. I can't say that I do every single one of these every single day, but my aspiration is to do at least one every day.

- Meditation or quiet contemplation
- Affirmation
- Reading inspirational material or listening to inspira-

tional material

- Journaling
- Using oracle cards
- Visualization
- Yoga
- Exercise
- Time in nature
- Time in the water

These are just a few examples. What are some processes that you use to help keep that focus on living your optimal life? Which ones have you found work best for you? How often do you use these processes or tools? What is the outcome in your life that you notice when you do or don't do your processes? What difference do you see as you deepen your practice?

This leads right into the next area of focus for me when it comes to living my optimal life, which is PRACTICE.

Dr. Chopra talks about being the eye of the hurricane as being able to be really calm *(still)* even when things around you are shifting or perhaps not going in a way that would be considered optimal. This is a reason I think that the "practice" piece is so important. Funny joke: I was hearing about a study that was done recently that showed that doing one bicep curl actually is helpful for improving your health and wellness, and I laughed because I thought, *Okay, and now people are going to think all they need to do is just one bicep curl and they're going to be ripped like Dwayne "The Rock" Johnson.*

The truth is practice is important. I can't say that my life goes optimally every single day because I do one of my processes every day, but what I can say is that on the days when I do my processes, I find it easier to be the eye of the hurricane. I find that when life's ups and downs show up, I'm able to handle the situations or solutions come to me with more clarity than on the days when I haven't paid attention to my processes. And there's more to that: as I deepen my practice, as I do my processes more and more, I get more experience, and so handling the rough patches becomes easier. It's not that the rough patches don't show up; it is part of life, but the rough patches don't steal my joy the way they used to.

I couldn't have this conversation without talking about PERSONAL CARE. I mean, for work, I do help patients with their health and wellness all day long!

The first suggestion that I would make has to do with your own mental health and wellness. I focus here first because I find that when I take care of that piece first, my own self-care, self-love, and self-appreciation, then the other factors that contribute to living an optimal life seem to fall into place easier. It seems as though in moments when difficulties arise, I'm still able to keep hold of joy.

Then, there is taking care of the physical body:

- Be sure to get enough sleep
- Stay hydrated
- Eat healthful foods in a mindful way
- Move your body in a way that is right for you
- Add in supplementation that is appropriate for your age stage and health status
- Listen to your body
- Seek professional help when needed

The last area of focus for me is PEOPLE.

When we talk about people, we are talking about our friends and family. You can't choose who your family is, but you can choose how you set your boundaries—what you allow, how you allow people to treat you, and how you train people to treat you. This applies to the people that you work with as well. When considering the people in your life, I like to think of the way we interact with each other as being a bit of a collaboration. So, my five rules for collaborations apply here.

Firstly, there is always an opportunity to ask for divine guidance when attempting to optimize relationships with our friends, family, co-workers, etc. Secondly, we always want to ensure that our relationships are in alignment with our values and our purpose. Thirdly, we want to make sure that there is give-and-take in the relationships. That we are all in, but also that other people that we are in relationship with—our friends, our families, our co-workers—that they appreciate that give-and-take dynamic and that they are all in also. Fourthly, we want to make sure that we're not doing all the things in the relationship but allowing others to give to us. We have to allow others to do the things that are their brilliance. We have to allow ourselves to receive and focus on the areas where we excel. Finally, when it comes to relationships and the people in our lives, there are always so many resources that are out there that can help us to live our optimal lives in relationships. We might find guidance or support from books, coaches, therapists, podcasts, or other applications. I have found that there is always information somewhere that can help us optimize the way we relate with each other.

This may be a bit controversial, but I truly believe that we're here to be amazing. I believe that we're here to have absolutely amazing lives and to enjoy this existence. I am convinced that we are here to wake up every single day and feel joy. I appreciate that there are times when things that show up seem less than optimal, and I also know that those times in my life have been some of the greatest opportunities for learning and growing. So, may I invite you to be the example, be the beacon of a life that is full of joy? Aspire and endeavor to live a life you're proud of, a life you're grateful for every day, because, in living your optimal life, you help others live their optimal life, too.

Selah

Integration

Optimal Life Star

I invite you to find a comfortable spot and close your eyes. Take a deep breath in, hold the breath, and then exhale. Let's do it again: take a deep breath in, hold the breath, and then go ahead and exhale. And one last time, take a deep breath in, hold the breath, and exhale all the way out, letting go of any holdups, any negativity, anything that might be holding you back from living your optimal life—just go ahead and breathe it all out.

I want you to imagine with your eyes closed that you're walking down a path in a beautiful forest. You come to a point in the path, and there's a beautiful bench and in front of the bench is set up an outdoor flat-screen large TV. You have a seat on this bench, and as you look at the TV, you notice that playing on the TV is your life. But this doesn't look exactly like the life that you know; it's better, it's brighter, it's more in focus, it's more vivid, it's more brilliant. Just think about what that looks like.

- Imagine that you're seeing your romantic life: What does your romantic relationship look like in this optimal life that you are seeing playing out in front of you on this TV screen?

- As you watch, take a deep breath in and exhale as the scene changes to show you what your life looks like as far as your family relationships and your relationships with your friends. In this optimal life picture, what's showing up for you here? What are you seeing?

- As you continue watching the big screen, the picture shifts to focus on your financial life. What does your ideal financial picture look like?

- The picture on the big screen shifts, and you're looking at your health, your well-being, and your wellness. What does that look like for you? What does that feel like?

- And one more time, the picture on the big screen shifts to focus on your spiritual life. What does that look like?

The pictures on the screen begin to fade. I invite you to take a deep breath, breathing in the energy of those pictures, in joy and gratitude, inviting those pictures to integrate themselves into your life. Then, imagine arriving back in the present moment. Take a deep breath in, and hold and exhale. Once more, take a deep breath in, hold that breath, and exhale. Finally, take one last deep breath in, hold, and then exhale.

Take out your journal and write some notes about what came up for you as you were watching yourself living your optimal life on that TV screen in your mind.

- What did each aspect of your life look like?

- What are some ideas that are coming to you about how your life can be closer to this optimal vision?

- What obstacles appear to be in your way?

- How can you overcome or utilize that perceived obstacle to get closer to living your best life?

About Dr. Davia

"In living your optimal life, you help others live their optimal life, too."

Dr. Davia H. Shepherd wears a lot of hats. She is a mom, a sister, a daughter, and a wife. She helps her patients feel better every day. Davia is a bestselling author and a professional speaker and coordinates our women's collaboration collective Ladies Power Lunch - LPL. The thing that she is most passionate about is the opportunity to support women in business to live their optimal lives: to grow their visibility, reach, impact, and income.

Davia is an amplifier. She has almost two decades of experience (in the corporate world as well as running her own community practice) with her innate ability to translate the energetic signature of the best version of you, into words. That big dream that you didn't even know you had, for both your business and your life? She not only can translate that for you, but also makes it bigger, using it to develop a solid plan for increased visibility, reach, and success. The result is that you shine your light at its most brilliant; that you stop being the world's best-kept secret. Your optimal clients, the ones who are losing sleep at night because they need you, the ones who light up when you work together, are then able to find you with ease and grace; and you can live your passion, be seen, be heard, and be visible.

Connect with Dr. Davia:
www.growsmarternotharder.com

CHAPTER 2

YOUR MAGNIFICENT SELF: GIVING BIRTH TO THE REAL YOU

ILJA VAN DE GRIEND

"Now what?"

I fought to hold back my tears, not wanting to wake up my husband, whose breathing next to me was the only sound in the silence of the night. The silence gave space to my inner demons that haunted me.

"What if your best years are already behind you? What will you do with your life? Will it still hold meaning? Will you still have any value? How will you earn any money to live?"

The tears that wanted to come were a mixture of sadness and anger for what I had lost: a planned future in which ambitious Ilja would be wildly successful and live the life of her dreams. Instead, I had found myself stopped in my tracks by a health challenge at 28 years old, making the road I was on a dead-end one. Trapped in a body full of pain, my cherished independence was replaced by a sense of shame. I dreaded the days because they reminded me of everything I had lost. And I dreaded the nights because they gave way to my worst enemy, a deep sense of unworthiness trying to swallow me up.

As I tried to focus on my own breathing in an attempt not to let the panic get hold of my brain and hijack me into the valley of despair, a thought appeared out of nowhere. Like a ray of light entering the inner and outer darkness I was experiencing myself in, a voice in my head whispered, "You just have to trust that there is more inside of you that you don't know yet, that has been dormant until now."

A sense of peace instilled itself in me, and I just knew I would be all right. I decided to give that inner voice a chance to show me the way and stop resisting my situation. The part of me that was furious that she, against her will, was stuck in this physically and emotionally dark place, feeling utterly impotent to make it go away, took a breath of relief. Maybe there is a tomorrow that I will be born into that will fill me again with joy and meaning. A sense of hope carried me back into dreamland for a few more hours of sleep, from which I awoke refreshed. I´m back on track! I can orient myself to a renewed sense of direction, not set by "my goals and ambitions" but rather by this mysterious inner voice that I am longing to get to know better. The inner voice feels like my ally like she is really on my side and knows me better than I know myself. And she speaks with such gentle conviction like she is so certain in the truth of what she says that there is no need to convince or force.

As I got out of my bed and started to get ready for the day, I hardly noticed the reality of the pain and limitations of my body. I had already begun expanding into this other reality to which she invited me, following the trail of her words that there is more inside of me than I know. If only that 28-year-old me could have seen into the future to witness her future self, I would have fought less hard to try to hold on to what was, resisting the transformation that was wanting to happen. Then again, until this visit of my inner voice, I did not believe I had it in me to rebuild my life, following my heart and inner knowing. That I could learn to blindly trust guidance, shed the layers of insensitivity that I had built up as a defense against traumatic experiences, and uncover my authentic, passionate, and compassionate self underneath the trauma imprints and conditioning. After that night, when I felt found, a happier period followed, in which I stopped trying to figure out what to do. And even if I felt my life had been okay as it was, I by now knew there was something "better" wanting to emerge. For that to happen, all I could do was to grow in trust and surrender to the journey I was on, and so I did. A summer passed, my health improved, my days got filled with more joy, and inner relaxation allowed me to be more in myself.

And then, as the summer gave way to September, the call to take the next step came loud and clear. As I was sitting outside, enjoying the late September sun, I just knew I had to start a regression therapy training I had recently learned about. My mind, by now used to not enter in fear and resistance, immediately got out of the way, and I called to find out the course would start in two weeks. There was one place left, and I simply knew it was my place. The next chapter was about to start, a year after my body had put me on pause. I was excited! I did not know when I put down the phone that my health challenge would turn out to be the biggest blessing in disguise of my life. Because when I, a month into the training, facilitated my first session as a therapist, that same body that had felt so much pain over the last year vibrated in a sense of ease, security, and satisfaction unknown to me. I had found Me! Looking back 24 years later, it seems everything unfolded by itself from that moment on. I learned to ride the wave of change in that first year after having received what now I would say was a wake-up call from my soul. My inner knowing brought me on the right path for me, and as I kept following its guidance, my life was transformed as my health improved. It led me first to become a therapist, then a coach and a healer. It led me through a divorce and landed me in Portugal with a Portuguese man.

Together, we founded Almasoma, the Lisbon-based transpersonal training institute, 17 years ago. Alma means soul in Portuguese, and Soma means body in Greek. We train therapists in a 4-year Transpersonal Psychotherapy training. Our intention is to help the soul embody and to facilitate the awakening to your transpersonal dimension while grounding down strongly into your body and this realm. Currently, we have 65 active students in training or supervision, supported by a team of 17 co-teachers, supervisors, and didactic psychotherapists. The inner voice sure did live up to her promise that there would be more inside of me that I didn't know yet, that had been dormant until now. As I went through the different courses and did the personal process that comes with that, and as I facilitated the sessions of my clients and observed those of my students, I started to wake up from a trance-like state.

With the fog clearing from my mind and the wall around my heart, desensitizing my heartbreak, dissolving, I started to realize that we are born as conscious, sensitive, magnificent beings. And that we are much more impacted by the experiences we have while in the womb of our mother and during and right after our birth than overall presumed. As we try to communicate the hurt in our body and heart via our crying and dysfunctional behavior, we are usually met with a lack of understanding and empathy. Our biological need for connection to feel safe in our body is discarded, as sleeping in our own room right from the start seems to be the highest good. Our innate capacity to heal from traumatic, destabilizing experiences by expressing, in relationship, through our crying, what is inside of us is stolen from us as we need to navigate a world of numbed adults. And most tragic of all, we are not seen for who we really are. The inner spark we bring is missed. Instead, there seems to be this vicious attempt to get us educated and socialized. At age 32, a year and a half into my regression therapy training, I became a mother for the first time. Following my inner knowing, I envisioned a way of parenting that would honor my daughter´s need for connection and support her in staying connected to her authentic self. I learned about the importance of release crying, where the baby, in connection with a caring adult, is allowed to cry to liberate inner tensions related to their pre- and perinatal and day-to-day experiences. As I sat with my daughter in my arms, holding space for her to release through her crying what was causing disharmony, it was like I had opened Pandora's box as a deep pain jumped on me like a black panther and nailed me to the floor. Gasping for air, I tried to find my breath and feet as I was looking at my daughter through my own tears. I was not anesthetized anymore, yet it would take me quite some years, integrating many more teachings and transformation techniques, to enter that deep, dark dungeon without fear and find the ground under my feet in there. It is that place where your vulnerability is met with complete indifference and violent acts, and there is nothing you can do to defend yourself, leaving you at the disposal of the forces around you. It is that place where you are treated as a non-human and not seen for the aware, magnificent being that you are. That's two strikes against you, and you have not yet started. As the years passed, my deepening journey into motherhood gave fuel to my own transformation. By the time my third daughter, born at home in a beautiful waterbirth, was a few months old, I was struck by how rock-solid our connection felt. In comparison to the connection with her sisters, both born in the hospital, there was a deep sense of trust and a natural sense of "us" present that I had not experienced before. I knew she had received a good start, with immediate and uninterrupted skin-to-skin contact for over an hour, delayed cord-cutting, breastfeeding on demand, and co-sleeping. But to see the ripple effect of that good start was eye-opening.

Feeling the longing to deepen my understanding of the impact of our pre- and perinatal experiences, I went to study Birth Psychology to become a Prenatal and Perinatal Educator and learned how to help babies heal their traumatic pre- and perinatal experiences.

It has been my experience with babies that really drove home the point my inner voice on that dark night 24 years ago made as it came to bring me home within. As I listened to parents sharing the story of what happened during the pregnancy and birth, and we tried to feel how it must have been for their baby, these babies seemed to be aware that we were trying to understand them, communicating through sounds and relieved looks that we were understanding them. As they were allowed to process the traumatic pre- and perinatal experiences, in contact with their parents, through release crying, I was stunned to see the look in their eyes change. From distant, withdrawn, distrustful, sad, angry, or defeated, they shifted to become present, calm, shining, open, curious, and joyful.

Now, ten years after I started exploring the impact of our pre- and perinatal experiences, I can say without any doubt that if we go within and shed the layers of trauma and conditioning, we uncover our magnificence buried underneath it, still intact, simply waiting to be recognized. It is in our primary period, that period from preconception up to the end of the first year of life after birth, that foundations are being laid that are found to have a life-long impact on all aspects of the human being—physical, emotional, mental, and spiritual. Many diseases and dysfunctionalities have their origin in this primary period, and the roots of violent behavior can be traced back here as well. So, if we want to live our optimal life, it makes sense to start by building ourselves a solid foundation from which we can rise and shine. Nowadays, there are so many amazing holistic healing and transformation approaches that help you bring your focus inward, get in touch with your body and feelings, heal your trauma, develop your intuition, reclaim your capacity to sense, create, and be in the moment, help you find your voice, contact your spirit guides, open your heart and what not.

I have experienced many of those approaches, and here is what I found—it all starts with you—choosing to give yourself a chance to have a life with more inner quality. To pursue well-being, not well-doing. To believe that you can experience bliss just sitting on a bench, breathing the air, feeling the sun on your skin, and hearing the birds sing. That you can live with a sense of peace and love in your heart no matter your outer experiences. When you make that choice, you can trust that the right person to help you take your next step will show up on your path. I don´t believe there is one approach superior to another—one teacher, coach, therapist, or healer is better than the other. There is only the right one for you at the right time.

But most importantly, you have You. And the You in you communicates with you through your inner knowing. If you listen to her and courageously follow her trail, she will guide you to be at home in yourself, in the company of peace and bliss.

Integration

- If the You in you would have any message for you right now, what would that be?

- Do you trust your inner knowing? Can you commit to listening to your inner voice? If not, what is in the way of that, and what would you need to be able to trust and surrender?

- Look at a picture of yourself as a baby (or close your eyes and imagine yourself as the baby you were). Look into your eyes, the window to your soul, and connect with the conscious being that you are. What does your higher mind know? What is your highest truth? What is the purpose of your life? Bring that higher vibration into your physical body and let it dissolve any non-truths that you are holding. Let your cells align with this higher vibration, with the truth of who you are, and let go, through your breathing, anything that no longer makes sense to you. Create space in your body to Be, breathing in that vibration of unconditional love and peace, breathing out any toxicity, fear, anger, or sadness that you are aware of. Know that you are more loved and held than you may experience to be true.

About Ilja

"If we go within and shed the layers of trauma and conditioning, we uncover our magnificence buried underneath it, still intact, simply waiting to be recognized."

Originally trained as a business economist and manager, a health challenge at 28 years old was a wake-up call to **Ilja van de Griend**'s soul. Since then, she has been on a path of (trans)personal development that led her to integrate therapy-, coaching- and healing modalities. She has been facilitating individual transformation journeys for 20 years and teaching therapists for almost as long. Over the past decade, she delved into the profound effects of our pre- and perinatal experiences, as well as our transgenerational legacy, inspired by her journey into motherhood. Her exploration led her to a deep understanding of their influence on our innate potential, bodies, relationships, and our way of parenting and leading. She realized that it is in our very early life that we lose the connection with our soul and inner knowing as we start to resonate with our family field, perpetuating transgenerational patterns. It was her wish to see her three daughters shine bright, that motivated her to go deep in her own healing journey and alchemize her (transgenerational) traumas into unconditional love and inner peace.

Currently, she offers online individual programs and group retreats to support you in your process to give birth to your real self. By holding the frequency of your magnificent soul-self, she is calling you forward on your hero´s journey. She catalyzes your process by accompanying you within to the depths of your individual, transgenerational, and collective wounds to find your gold, rise, and share your magnificence with the world.

Connect with Ilja:
Almasoma Transpersonal Institute
www.almasoma.pt
www.iljavandegriend.com
Email: ilja@almasoma.pt

You can download the audio version of the Integration Questions here:
https://bit.ly/YourMagnificentSelf

Chapter 3

Self-Love is the Foundation of an Optimal Life

Mary Ann Francis, LMFT

Reflecting back on who I was once, I never imagined that I would be where I am today. Everyone has their story and their own personal journey. I am grateful for mine despite the challenges. It wasn't until later in life that I realized you can't get to the top of a mountain without climbing it first. Now, some of us already know that because of what we were taught, and others, well—they pretty much found out the hard way. The unfortunate part is that some people never get to see the top because they've become so exhausted from life's bruises that they have given up on the notion that life can get better. Call me an optimist, but I am a firm believer that it can. Sometimes, you have to work harder than others to obtain your peace and happiness, and others may not have to work as hard. Either way, when you become an adult—you choose. You choose if you love yourself enough to give yourself the life you deserve.

I was a teenage mother. Learning, coping, trying to figure out adulthood, motherhood, attending college full-time, working part-time, and just trying to live life. When I gave birth to my daughter at 19, I knew that I had no other choice but to look forward and accomplish my goals. My goal at the time was to obtain my PsyD. However, needing to transfer out of my university in New York to be closer to home, my goals had to change slightly to adjust to having a baby. What also was different for me was being in a relationship. My first "serious" relationship, alongside the fact that I was a mother. When you are trying to navigate who you are based on what you have learned in your upbringing, it's difficult to grasp the full understanding of what it all means and how it should all go. Especially at such a young age when you haven't figured out who you are yet.

My thought at the time was that, in those moments, all that mattered was the family I had. Growing up in a two-parent household, my father was the head, and my mother was the neck. So, I grew up with the concept that one without the other could never balance or have support. What I would soon find out was that not everyone's household had the same concept or had two-parent households. People truly go by what they have experienced or their concept of how things should be. My dad worked two jobs, took care of the yard, took care of his parents who lived next door to us, and made sure he was coaching us through the sports we were signed up for. Since I saw my mother take care of the house, for example, chores, cooking, and work, that's what I did.

At that time, since I was still in school, my contribution to finances was minimal, but I did what I could. My daughter's father took care of the household bills, including rent, and he worked hard at it. Initially, I thought things were going well. But little things here and there made me feel uncertain if this was how things were supposed to be or not. Small things such as jealousy, which initially I thought was "cute" as a way that he showed he loved me. But then, I grew to feel controlled. Never wanting me to go and have fun with my friends. Now, there are some mothers who believe that you should be home at all times with your kids. Going out and having fun is the sacrifice you made when you had children. The thing is, I was still a teenager, and I was still being responsible by going to school, working, and taking care of the household. So, why not enjoy some time with your friends? This turned into a guilt trip every time I went out. I couldn't fully enjoy my time with friends because I was receiving messages that only made me want to go back home.

After a while, I stopped going out with my friends. However, that didn't stop him from going out or having his friends over every day. I noticed that my unhappiness grew, and the distance between us grew greater. I got to the point where a part of me no longer trusted some of his decisions because I realized they weren't great decisions. So, often, I reverted back to my parents as a source of knowledge. I began turning to my parents more and more and realized he was not okay with that. Understandably, he felt that I didn't trust his guidance, and quite honestly, I didn't. But it wasn't just that. If I didn't agree with what he said, he felt betrayed. Regardless if he was wrong, it was the concept of thinking "the world against me." I simply couldn't understand this. I felt that I couldn't have an opinion. It was suffocating.

Tension grew. Every day, his friend would come over, and dinner was no longer for three but for four. There was no quality time, no self-care time, and lots of stress. Eventually, we moved in with my parents due to financial reasons.

Sometimes, small blessings come without you realizing it. This move would be the place I stayed for the next seven years as I built my life without him. About six months after our move, he moved out of my parents. His leaving was the best decision for us. Although I was concerned and hurt about my daughter not having a two-parent household, the relationship was just not working.

During the breakup, I endured so much emotional abuse. According to him, I wasn't a good mother, I wasn't a good girlfriend, I was worthless—ugh, the belittling was exhausting. I often didn't feel good enough. I didn't feel pretty enough. I often felt alone.

My motherly instinct to not want to let go of my child was difficult. A custody "battle" was what he wanted, and it was excruciating. I don't understand, to this day, why anyone would want to make a process like that so excruciating. I learned that what could have been a visitation plan was more of an ego trip. A way to cause hurt and pain versus actually doing what was best for our child. The amount of anger that was there didn't make sense to me because, hell, I didn't leave the relationship. But everything seemed to be my fault. I didn't ask for child support, but he volunteered, and yet that was my fault. It didn't make sense.

It wasn't until after my post-grad training that I realized that "battle" wasn't about me. That battle was his own childhood demons. Something that he had never healed from. And yet, despite the tumultuous five years of enduring back-and-forth court proceedings over petty things, I continued my education.

Between the ages of 20 and 25, I centered around building up myself. I became what others saw as "cold." In reality, I just began to choose myself. After all the years of not feeling good enough, I had to remind myself where I was going and what I was presently doing to get there. Loving myself was the light that carried me through the dark times. My daughter was the constant reminder that failure was never an option. This was the only way I felt I could survive. Choosing me. Loving myself. Believing in myself. Trusting myself.

Because despite what was happening, my daughter was watching.

Getting my bachelor's degree was one of my biggest accomplishments during that time. It gave me confidence and the ability to know that I can do it despite the odds. So, I continued to plan what my next moves were, and that included going to graduate school. I chose to take up Marriage and Family Therapy to gain an understanding of how to deal with such a crippling dynamic. As a young mother, I didn't understand everything that was happening. All I knew was that I had to take care of my daughter, and if I wanted the best life not only for her but to keep my dreams alive, I had to keep moving forward.

My degree in Marriage and Family Therapy taught me several things. But the one thing that still resonates to this day, even when facilitating sessions, is that people choose if they want to change. I cannot change anyone. I began to live life moving forward, knowing that. Regardless of who I encounter, I am taking them for who they show me they are, not who I want them to be. When we speak about optimal life, this is part of that journey. Loving yourself and seeing things/people for what they are. Self-love is the foundation of creating your optimal life.

My journey isn't about who did what. It's truly about understanding the lessons, gathering the information I have learned, and applying it to my life moving forward. My current experience doesn't look the way it once did, but that's because I heeded the life lessons. I chose and continue to choose to live my life unapologetically. I chose to align myself with the things that I desired, even when I didn't know exactly where it would lead.

What does optimal life mean to me? It means that there are times when I have to let go of the things that no longer serve me, regardless of how difficult it may be. It means choosing that I know myself better than anyone else does, and that means I acknowledge all of the imperfections as well. It means I have to continue to be a listener not only to what is said but also to what is not said. And trust. Trust that no matter what, the universe will lead me to where I need to be, even when I can't see it. Trust myself to make the decisions that will be best for me.

Now I've heard people say, if you're doing everything for yourself, isn't that selfish? Absolutely not. When I started making choices for myself and doing what was best for me, ultimately, it was also best for my daughter. Because of this, she received the best parts of me as I continued to heal from the parts of me that were hurt. I stopped denying my parts that were hurt. I stopped hiding them and began embracing them as part of my journey because that is self-love. Embracing the perfect and imperfect parts. Embracing the good memories and embracing the challenges. Doing this led me to the life I have now with a loving husband and a career I am passionate about. A great relationship with my daughter. And a network of positive support surrounding me. Simply because I was willing to let go of what once was and continued to show up for myself with compassion, forgiveness, and love.

Self-love is the foundation. My self-love is unapologetic.

Integration

- How can you begin to embrace your imperfect parts and the parts that you love?
- What have been the lessons in life you learned that you have chosen to embrace?
- What does self-love mean to you?

About Mary Ann

"Self-love is the foundation. My self-love is unapologetic."

Mary Ann Francis is a Licensed Marriage and Family Therapist in Connecticut. The inspiration for her work continues to be driven by her desire to help people live their lives unapologetically. Mrs. Francis not only helps couples thrive and find their authentic selves through therapy work but also helps her consumers heal energetically through Reiki and through The Self-Love movement called UNA-pologetically™. She has also built teen workshops and a school curriculum to help teenagers find their path to self-love. As a Latina, it is important to Mrs. Francis that this work continues in all communities, especially black and brown communities.

Connect with Mary Ann:
Mending Hearts LLC
www.mendingheartsct.com
Email: info@mendingheartsct.com

Chapter 4

A Design Discovery

Annette Stahl Farha

A pea-sized nuisance changed my life forever. Spoiler alert: it wasn't because I was a princess sitting atop a million mattresses.

At age 43, I was a divorced mom of 15- and 12-year-old boys. I was also juggling building a real estate team along with project managing, designing, and drafting new homes that aligned with my clients' dream lives. Driven and determined, I felt sure that if I just kept hustling, I would be happy *when* I made my goal weight, or *when* my vision board came to life, or *when* I automated my systems, or *when* the gorgeous, comfy couch and the colorful, fluffy rug arrived for us all to pile on and play games like those happy families on sitcoms. I was in the race for happiness built on "*when I finally...*" a hare running after a carrot suspended somewhere on the horizon. That "*when I finally...*" kept me hustling, going faster and faster, and saying yes to more and more in hopes of safety, certainty, and fulfillment.

During this period of hustling, I had an amazing soul connection and love with my life partner. We collaborated in business and life while keeping our own separate abodes. I loved my colorful, creative, eclectic sanctuary for my boys and me, and he loved his space his way. He'd often visit by sliding into my bed after dark when everyone else was snuggled asleep in theirs and then leave for his bagel and coffee before the sun even peaked over the horizon.

One hot morning in August, he woke up with a pea-sized hard spot on his arm. He told me he planned to have his doctor check it out to ensure his winning golf swing would be ready for his tournament weekend.

That evening, he texted me to meet him at an unfamiliar address for dinner. When I was almost there, I realized it was the emergency room. We found out the pea-sized hard spot was a blood clot caused by acute myelogenous leukemia, or AML for short. The world as we knew it changed forever. To live, he had to start treatment within the next three days. The treatment had a very low survival rate and required 30-day isolation at MD Anderson in Houston, Texas, which was states away from us. All of a sudden, my hustle shifted from chasing dreams to staying alive.

Since both of us were business-building entrepreneurs with five companies between us, the diagnosis sent me into "go mode" to redesign our calendars. I started with the four Ds: what could we delegate, what could we delay, what could we dump, and then what did we have to do to survive? He had seven kids from his first marriage, with three still at home, and I had my two boys. My head was playing the Bee Gees on repeat: *"Ah, ah, ah, ah, stayin' alive, stayin' alive."* I felt both the dark, empty anxiety of aloneness and this burning fire of purpose to focus on moving the mountain before us to attain our dream life.

If this is our last day, then how much love can we have, and how much fun can we make it?

The little girl in me wished there was someone coming to rescue me, while my inner independent teen was sure that all I had was myself. His need for me and my love invigorated my inner hero and propelled me to action.

Our second priority was protecting our kids, which meant maintaining our sales and income to keep roofs over our heads and food in our bellies. What was the 20 percent of our actions that returned 80 percent of our revenue? What work could give us the biggest payback? Brutal prioritization hurt. I felt my gut tighten as I imagined an angry mob of disappointed clients blowing up my voicemail, text, and email for letting them down. My greatest fear was failing to be enough, and here I was, choosing to do the least possible work with the greatest payback to focus on us. Choosing me was wobbly. I felt like Bambi trying to walk on ice for the first time.

Stretching myself to please others would have cost me my vitality, which he needed most as he fought for his life. So, I embraced the wobble. Bringing a big breath of life in and exhaling the rest, I got down to the business of cutting all non-essentials. Our businesses needed to support us instead of the other way around. I wrote emails and texts as we boarded the plane for MD Anderson, 750 miles away from our Kansas-centered businesses, kids, and homes.

Years before, I buried my bare toes into the dirt where our home stood to ask Mother Earth for her desire. The blueprint that dropped in fit on this odd-shaped lot by an inch. Our home and sanctuary came to life from that blueprint.

The design featured a sidewalk curving around the front to our porch on the corner. From the entry, you could peek into the living, dining, and kitchen. The vibrant colors, walls of windows with views of nature's green grasses and trees, and exposed beams kept visitors' attention in our main space and away from more cluttered areas.

I was a realtor who designed, drafted, and marketed new homes. The outside world saw me with my people-pleasing smile in magazine-perfect model homes building the top real estate team. I kept our messy, colorful, playful, eclectic home as a private sanctuary just for us.

Anyone attempting to venture into our messy, private spaces would be met with a forced smile and a *"Hold on, let me grab that in the pantry"* as I slipped in and closed the door promptly.

Or a *"Wait! That's just my laundry room and master closet, so nothing to see."*

Or a *"Whoa, hold your horses! That may look like a coat closet door, but if you open it, be ready for an avalanche!"*

Or an *"Of course, you can borrow that art supply, stay right here at the front door, and I'll go grab it!"*

The craft room looked like a tornado hit the crafting section of a *Michael's* store.

I shifted from working at home in my design center, available to my boys 24/7, to working 750 miles away in the blink of an eye.

My clients experienced my curious questions about their desires and dreams while touring their homes. Why? Because our outer spaces reflect our inner spaces. While I knew this, the reality of my mess being exposed left me pressing my eyes closed and holding my breath as I reluctantly let out a whisper for help.

What will they think? Who will love my messiness? How will this work?

I discovered freedom in coming undone. I discovered breathing space. By being my raw and real self, my loved ones felt safe enough to be raw and real for me, which allowed for deeper connections. Instead of my energy being spent holding things together, I discovered I was a woman with range who could allow others to be whole, complete humans with their experience of me and my designs without melting over their judgment like the Wicked Witch of the West. Opening up to ask for support was challenging and a transformational wake-up call.

Every day, I intentionally chose to love more and live like it was my last day. I redefined success as how much fun we were having. Instead of my mess being something wrong with me, it showed me my cravings, desires, and where I could ask for support. I needed to understand my mess so I could self-nourish and fill my cup. My motivation as a caregiver needed to be love and joy, not depletion, resentment, or exhaustion.

My life partner and I discovered that focusing on connections and loving people shifted us from human doers to human beings. This deep intimacy arose in this space of being present to play and connect. He was hooked to machines, looking like a pin cushion, with all kinds of beeping as they adjusted his treatments. His body reacted with rashes, swelling, vomiting, random bleeding, and more. By being present in the moment, choosing to love more, and settling into our breath, we could shift how our space felt and even affect his blood pressure. I called it our "Glenda the Good Witch Soft Twinkly Pink Love Sphere."

Our bodies, our environment, our emotions, and our energy are intertwined.

When we choose to connect, we open ourselves up to magical possibilities. The interconnection and power of presence and intention became so clear to me. This clarity opened a whole new space that sparked the fire in me to inspire others to be free to create their life by their own design. Allowing the flame of their desires and dreams to melt their self-built cages, the ones that hold us in proving and performing instead of being free to be our real messy wholehearted, imperfectly perfect selves.

While we were blessed with a remission, AML came back and won the second round. He always said I was his forever and he was my "for right now." His greatest wish was to love me and share my light and love. He'd say, "The world needs you to be your *you-est you* to light it up and spread your laugh and passion."

What surprised me most at MD Anderson was the expansive joy. These beautiful souls deal with so much pain and loss, yet they find joy in the connection and love with those holding their hands. While chatting with a few nurses, they shared with me the greatest regrets they'd heard from their patients. One of the most common was lacking the courage to live a life true to their heart's desire and wishing they'd had more time to connect, play, and love those in their life.

After designing, drafting, and building over 400 homes, I find deep connection and joy in holding space for my clients to become clear on how they desire their lives to function, feel, and flow. I had a couple struggling through fertility treatments share their dream for a new home out in nature on a plot closer to her parents and sister. Together, we gained clarity on their dream so we could clear the space to bring it to life. They chose to take a break from fertility treatments for a year to focus on their dream home. A few months after living in their new home, they called me to share that they were pregnant with twins and never even had to go back on the fertility treatment roller coaster. To witness the birth of their dream life was a beautiful moment.

Another couple had just launched their youngest child out of the nest into adulthood and desired to find each other again as a couple instead of just parents. We created a space for them to refinish and build furniture together. Over time, their shared passion for carpentry connected them in a new, deeper way. They turned their shared passion into a profitable business, opening the opportunity for them to travel and check off some of their bucket list destinations.

How can you shift your space and life?

First, become clear on what is annoying or frustrating in your space. If you feel overwhelmed by the entire space, then just pick a shelf or drawer in the space.

Take a big belly breath in and hold it. When it gets tight, exhale everything not in this moment until it feels like it's all released, and then push your exhale out even more. Now, repeat this, releasing belly breath two more times. Once you're grounded in this moment, go to the space you chose to work on.

How committed are you to acting?

Whatever comes up is perfect for you at this moment. Honor it. If you feel called, then get ready to act. If you feel like you need more time, then just keep reading to plant the seed for later.

What do you feel like in this space now?

How do you desire to feel? What is possible when you feel this desired feeling? For example, if you desire to feel loved and at peace in your bedroom, then what is possible when you feel loved and at peace? Maybe you sleep better and/or connect deeper with your partner or yourself.

Set an intention for your space.

It can be to open space for possibilities, clear the way for your dreams, open space for shifting, or for a specific feeling.

Now, look around and see what juices your energy. What makes you feel joyful or alive? Perhaps something bubbles up within you, saying, "I love this!" Now, look around the space, and maybe even put your hand on everything in the room. Assess each object. If it's neutral and used every day, then move on to the next item. If it zaps your energy or is not being used, then let it go. Thank it for its time and what it has done for you up to this point. Place it in a box or bag for donating or gifting. If it's unusable, recycle it if possible. If not, trash it.

Whatever you decide to do, your goal is to remove it from the space. No place to put it? Stick it in your vehicle until you can deliver it to its next loving home.

There is potency in commitment and action. Letting one thing go opens space for a shift. Even a broken pen makes space for more color in your world and more expression.

Celebrate your commitment to act to open space.

Take a big loving breath in and acknowledge your action. Hold the breath. Feel to fullness. Acting takes courage and is the beginning of change.

Without judging, just be an observer. What do you notice? How does the space feel? How does your body feel in this space? Are you feeling the urge to do more? Or just observe?

This is the work I do.

If you choose to work with me, we will first discover your discomfort, desire, and/or dream. How do you want your space to function? How do you want it to feel? How do you desire it to flow, both individually and with the spaces around it?

We dream. We may make a mood or vision board, or we may choose to write the story of our dream life. We co-create in the way that feels most aligned for you.

We clear and open space. Dreams expand when we open space for them.

Designing a home that is aligned with your values ensures a strong foundation for you to build your framework. Then we can start playing to see how it all functions, feels, and flows for you. I'll invite you to give yourself permission to play and discover how different arrangements and colors feel for you. We will explore nature's elements in your space and how they can create shifts and balance. My intent is to use all my life lessons, years of experience, and skills to inspire you to play and have fun with your space so you can align your inner and outer spaces to **live your life by your design**.

Integration

- What juices you? Lights you up?
- What zaps you? Drains or depletes how you feel?
- How can you add one juicer to your day? How can you eliminate one zapper from your day?

About Annette

"Dreams expand when we open space for them."

After a decade of corporate experience, **Annette Stahl Farha** emerged into entrepreneurship, building the top real estate team in her market. Excelling in seeing patterns and building systems, she developed Client's Choice to price and design a new home in one consultation. A Design Discovery designed, drafted, and built over 400 new homes, each one aligned with her clients' dream lives. Through weaving her clients' dreams with all her mind, body, and spirit practices, A Design Discovery aligns inner and outer spaces. As an intuitive designer, entrepreneur, and transformational leader, Annette will open the space you need to expand into YOUR life to live by YOUR design.

Connect with Annette:
https://adesigndiscovery.com/
https://linktr.ee/annettefarha

PART II

COURAGE

Chapter 5

The Inherent Gift

Wendy Wolpert

When war broke out in Ukraine in the Winter of 2022, it seemed so unreal. We were reliving events eerily familiar to what my family and six million Jews and other minorities experienced during World War II. The roots of both sides of my family are in Kyiv and Odessa, formerly part of Russia. It is now for the people of Ukraine to believe in miracles and to hold the vision of hope throughout the unknown and the unfathomable.

My maternal great-grandparents migrated and settled in Warsaw. My grandmother was one of six children. She was born in the early 1900s into a well-respected family of philanthropists. Her female relatives studied to become doctors, lawyers, and other highly educated professionals. She was introduced to my grandfather when she was a teenager by one of her brothers, and they fell in love.

Soon after, my grandfather received papers to leave Poland. He was given the choice to go to either Paris or America—he chose Paris. My grandmother followed her heart and eventually chose to be with my grandfather in Paris. It was a most beautiful time to be living the optimal life in Paris during the La Belle Epoque Era in the 1920s!

Somewhere along their magical journey, a man returned from Spain to his home in Paris. My grandfather would meet him randomly in La Place de la Republique. They were acquaintances who would frequent the same cafes, bonding over their love of French cigarettes. On one of these outings, this man was doodling on the paper cafe tablecloth they both shared. He asked if my grandfather would like to keep his doodle. At the time, my grandfather laughed, thinking his offer was silly, not realizing the identity of who he was sitting with.

When my grandfather recounted this story many years later, he paced the floor, rubbed his head, and lamented with a smile, *"Ahhh, if only I had known how famous that doodle was, I would have kept it!"* He discovered later that the man he had become acquainted with was Pablo Picasso.

My mother was born in 1926, and my aunt eight years later. To celebrate the birth of his second child, my grandfather bought a lottery ticket. A man who had recently moved from Argentina was sharing his troubles with my grandfather. Grandpapa showed him the lottery ticket, telling him not to worry and promising him half of the winnings if he won. Sure enough, Grandpapa won! In those days, 50,000 francs (my mother remembers, as she was seven years old) was quite a large sum. True to his word, even though my grandfather was hardly a wealthy man, he shared 50 percent of his winnings with the man.

My mother and aunt lived an idyllic childhood in Paris. My mother remembers with much fondness the music, singing and dancing with the accordion players, celebrating on the street corner every year on Bastille Day. My mother loved playing sports, bicycling, running, and playing soccer with groups of friends. She was fortunate enough to spend much of her teenage years hiding in captivity from the Nazis doing just that.

One day, while playing, they saw a large sign of a Fortune Teller—her friends jumped at the opportunity to check it out. The fortune teller took my mother's palm and saw that she would be taking a long trip across the ocean. She was told that when she arrived, she would meet a dark, handsome man. My mother laughed and said she didn't believe in fortune-telling.

Several years later, after the war ended, my mother did indeed travel across the ocean with 10,000 American soldiers and the famous designer Nina Ricci. She moved to New York, where eventually she was introduced to that dark, handsome man who would later become my father.

The life as they knew it had shifted forever in 1940 when the Germans invaded Paris. Antisemitism and bullying were on the rise for those who were required to wear the yellow star. When the German army officially arrived in Paris, my grandfather was called by the Surete Generale, the agency for safety and security at that time, to translate some requests from a German captain. The German captain and Grandpapa developed a rapport during this encounter.

One day in 1941, that same man, Captain Mueller, in his crisp black Gestapo uniform, knocked on the door of my grandparents' apartment with a *"Heil Hitler"* greeting. He said, *"I have a proposal for you."*

Can you imagine what was running through the minds of my grandparents? Jews were disappearing left and right in Europe at this time. What could he possibly be proposing?

Captain Mueller continued, *"I will change your identity papers to become a non-Jewish family of Aryan descent. You will have a different name so you can remain safely in Paris."*

My grandfather thanked Captain Mueller, and with utmost grace and gratitude, looking straight into his eyes, he replied, *"Thank you, Captain Mueller, I was born a Jew, and I will die a Jew."*

Captain Mueller gave him a warm embrace with much respect and replied, *"Then I will give you my private chauffeur and provide transportation for you to hide outside of Paris. I do not need to know where you are."*

Yes, it's really true, A German SS Officer provided transport for my family safely out of Nazi-occupied Paris to the safe environs of Normandy. Several years later, the Allies landed on June 6, 1944, to end the war, which coincided with my father's 18th birthday. As Carl Jung would say, there are no coincidences—only synchronicities.

Not only did my family receive this miraculous treatment—in fact, so many other Jews and minorities were saved by Captain Mueller that he was exonerated given his humanity after being put on trial when the war ended.

My grandfather was closely affiliated with La Surete Generale. It was an agency responsible for safety and security in Paris during the 1930s. He was able to keep track of the political state within Europe, as well as have the proper papers in place to move. When my beautiful, brilliant cousins arrived in Paris during the late 1930s to pursue higher education at La Sorbonne, my grandfather implored them not to return to Warsaw. They did not heed his warnings. To this day the story of what happened to all of my grandmother's warm, loving family is unknown. We had heard through word of mouth that my great-grandparents—and most likely other family members—had been killed early on in a raid. Of course, they were targeted as they had a prominent street in Warsaw named after them.

After much searching over the years, we could not find a trace of their whereabouts. I feel, however, that maybe somewhere, there are some who escaped, were able to make it through the war alive, and created a life somewhere in Europe. How wonderful it would be to find out.

The first place my family was taken to by Captain Mueller's chauffeur as a safe haven was a magnificent chateau. In the middle of the night, while they were all asleep, there was a knock at the door. A loud voice said *"Deutsche Polizei! We are here to take over this place."* Scared to death, my grandparents opened the door to let them in. My mother vividly remembers at 13 years old seeing her father's hair turning white.

Being Jewish, my grandparents spoke Yiddish, which is a language similar to German. The soldiers must have detected the difference, however, knowing they were Jewish. The German soldiers were surprised to see a family there. As they walked around, surveying the rooms of the chateau, they apologized respectfully, *"We're sorry we seem to have made a mistake. We do not wish to disturb a family who is living here with young children."* One of the soldiers, upon leaving, gave my mother a gift of a most gorgeous sparkling silver accordion.

When I heard her tell this incredible story of being so Divinely Protected, I felt the gift of this accordion symbolized their eventual independence and freedom. My mother was able to keep the accordion with her during hiding and brought it back to Paris after the war. My mother still sees the face of the German soldier who gave her that accordion.

After that incident, my grandfather felt it would be safer to move further into the countryside, to an area where it would be unlikely for the soldiers or police to want to take over the home. Through the grapevine, they heard of a group of farmers who had space and would be willing to provide a place for them to stay. One day, my grandfather was out and never came back. My mother frantically rode her bicycle through the unmanicured paths of trees and miraculously spotted him being interrogated by the French police. How she managed to find him in those woods was a feat of fierce determination. He motioned for her to leave so they would not see her.

When she returned safely to the farmers, they informed her a German soldier had been shot. As the police knew my grandfather was head of the local Resistance, they arrested him for questioning. Shortly thereafter, my grandmother went to the supermarket and never returned. My mother, 17 at that time, and her sister, age nine were left wandering in the French countryside with no place to go.

A farmer on a tractor called out to them, asking if they were the young girls whose parents had been arrested. My mother said no, and my aunt said yes. Out of the goodness of his heart, he offered to put them up, and the young girls found themselves once again living on another farm.

A month or so later, the French police arrived, inquiring where the girls were. They heard this farmer was housing them, and that he needed to surrender them. The man said he did not know where they were. The police said they had already sent my grandparents to a concentration camp, adding that they were most likely dead by now. My mother was about to let out a bloodcurdling scream when her younger sister silenced her so firmly by covering her mouth as they were hiding in the hot attic, with rats crawling all about. Although the police were searching in the very next room, they did not bother to look there. The police were satisfied the girls were not in the house and left.

When my aunt eventually came to this country, she graduated with honors from Columbia University. An opportunity later arose for her to work for the United Nations during the 1960s and beyond. She volunteered for many humanitarian missions and causes. My aunt Regine led an incredibly purposeful life traveling, immersed in various cultures. She helped to modernize and bring equality to many, primarily in Africa. Her friends were from all over the world. We grew up with an awareness of knowing a variety of beautiful people from different countries and cultures.

I am beyond grateful for my aunt's open-mindedness, expansive wisdom, vision, and generosity. Her intentional loving kindness to all, sense of adventure, love of the arts, her beautiful singing voice, and *joie de vivre* are just some of her many gifts.

August 3, 1944, was my mother's 18th birthday. The farmers asked what she wished for. The only thing she wished for was to have her parents back again.

Five days later, on August 8, one of the young farm boys was riding his bicycle eagerly towards my mother, calling *"Mademoiselle Rosine—your parents!"*

As my mother whirled around incredulously, lo and behold, she witnessed her beloved parents walking towards her, very much alive! It looked and felt like a mirage, yet it was real—everyone was crying with joy and jubilation! It was an incredible reunion and celebration!

They were never sent to the camps. The Allies had landed in Normandy, the police had fled the prison, and my grandmother somehow had gotten hold of the key and had released everyone in the prison. The police had confiscated the jewelry everyone had been wearing when arrested, yet before she left, Grandmama reached far back into the deep recesses of a desk drawer in the prison and found her ring. It felt like a miracle, and it was indeed another symbol of the strength and courage they had endured to remain alive and free.

When I was 12, graduating from elementary school, I was awarded the American Legion Medal for Leadership. The other attributes were Courage, Honor, Scholarship, Patriotism, and Service. One female and one male were chosen from the graduating class of 120 students. I felt surprised with humility when they called my name, yet incredibly excited and honored!

I remember my grandparents being there—they were so proud! They had a ring custom-made for me of a flower with a little Diamond inside.

Writing this story now, I have a much deeper understanding of why it meant so much to them for me to be recognized as a Leader for those qualities.

Years later, when my older daughter became a creative writer, without knowing the details of these stories, she wrote a poem with the title *"Inside The Heart Of A Flower."*

It is truly miraculous what gets passed on to each succeeding generation from the generations before. If only more of us would be curious to listen to the wisdom and inspiration from the memories and stories of our elderly relatives and ancestors so we could share these wonderful treasures.

After she left Poland, my rebellious grandmother did not go back to see her family out of fear. She left home at the age of 18 to follow her dreams against the wishes of her parents. It was a very bold and courageous move on her part, yet one which, unknowingly at the time, would save her life and the life of the family line. My grandma Ruta was truly the Sacred Rebel.

My mother did not have the opportunity to meet her grandparents, uncles, or aunts, one of whom was merely a year older than my mother. The fact that they all perished in a brutal way, along with the grief of three generations, has had a profound impact on me. I deeply wish I could heal them all. Growing up without knowing this warm, beautiful, loving family has created an indescribable gap in my life. Even as a young child, I was aware of that, although my grandparents did not speak of it.

At times, I could feel their presence as though I was hearing voices—looking under my bed, there was nothing, same for in the closet. So, where were these "voices" coming from? It would not be until years later that I would come to understand these were the voices of unprocessed grief, stories that had never been told and needed to be shared. By sharing these stories, so much spiritual energy of five generations is being witnessed, honored, and released. May their precious souls rest in peace.

With choking sensations welling up inside my throat, an internal voice says, *"I have to write. I owe it to my ancestors, to my own integrity of my mission of choosing to help heal others, to discover what is keeping them from living their optimal lives, and to guide them into creating the vision and tools for living their optimal lives."*

My mother is now nearly 97 years old. Her mind and memory are still remarkably intact. She is currently undergoing a mild form of chemotherapy as her red blood cells are fighting amongst themselves to stay alive and thrive within her body.

There is so much more to this story, some of which is still being written through the next generation.

I loved to read and write growing up. When I was nine years old, I wrote a book that my teacher was so enthusiastic about she suggested to my mother to follow through and have it published. She didn't.

Perhaps my message is that I am meant to follow through now as I share my stories with you. As long as the opportunities remain, it is not too late for that. It took me years, decades, to fully understand the magnitude of my mother's grief over her experiences.

There is a hidden child in me that wants to keep going and write so much more, yet I know for this chapter I must pause for now. I've discovered along this journey there is a hidden child in each and every one of us.

Integration

- Find some quiet time to meditate, engaging in activities you enjoy. While your mind is in a relaxed state, see if you can connect to your inner child. What is prominent or unusual that comes up about a time in your childhood memory? Find a journal and pen and start free-flow writing about it. Keep writing until you feel complete.
- When you are ready, read through your writing. Approaching it with a sense of curiosity and non-judgment, how are you feeling about what you wrote?
- What is the significance of your passage? How did this affect your life then? How is this affecting your life now? What did you learn from this experience?

About Wendy

"When we are attuned and respond to the needs of our hidden child within, we are able to live our lives to the fullest. To me, this is how to live an optimal life!"

Wendy Wolpert is a heart and soul-centered Certified Jungian life coach and abundance financial coach as a Certified Public Accountant (CPA). Wendy weaves these together to create real magic for dreams and visions to come to fruition.

Connect with Wendy:
Email: wisdomsbywendy@gmail.com or
wendywolpertcpa@gmail.com
You may set up a call with Wendy here:
https://calendly.com/wisdomsbywendy

Chapter 6

Facing Loss, Embracing Courage

Gail Petrowsky

I wake up, look over at the empty space, and feel a cold hard lump in my throat. Tears wet my face. My heart aches. The reality hits home. He is no longer here. I am alone. This really did happen.

The love of my life, my best friend, my lover, protector, my safe haven, the man I met at age 15 and was married to for 52 years, is gone forever! The shock of it is soul-shattering.

Joe worked out every day of his life. He was in the best shape. He was healthy, vitally alive, and fit, but despite all of this, he died unexpectedly on November 18th, 2022. I am fighting the reality that he is gone forever.

How did this happen? It was all so unexpected and incomprehensible.

We were planning on finally going away for two weeks for my 74th birthday. The plan was that Joe would work on his mortgage business for a brief period every day but still be on vacation with me. We were also making plans to spend our 53rd wedding anniversary in Greece, where we had celebrated our 25th together.

We were so happy and looking forward to all of this!

Instead, a few weeks before we were set to leave, Joe did not feel well.

We thought it was the flu. After a few days, he had a fever and passed out.

I called 911, and we raced to the hospital. After a few days, it was clear he was very ill, and we transferred him to a larger hospital. He was not getting better. The doctors discovered that a bacteria called streptococcus had entered his bloodstream and created a huge infectious mass in his liver. He also had sepsis. Between the septic shock, the stress of being so sick, and 12 days in the hospital, my guy had lost weight and strength and was forced to use a walker.

I was relieved when the doctors finally agreed that they had his infection under control and that Joe could leave the hospital with me. Joe was still very ill, but nurses would come to help us with his healing. He was tired of the hospital and couldn't wait. *"Get me out of here, Gail,"* is what he said.

On the way home, Joe looked at me and strangely said, *"Gail, you are strong emotionally and physically?"* I wondered, did he have a premonition of some kind? I could not understand why he said that to me at that moment.

He was so happy to be home. And I had my guy back!

He ate lunch and dinner, and we got into bed together. He reached out for my hand and said, *"I am so happy just being here holding your hand. I'm in heaven."*

The next morning, Joe told me he had the best sleep of his life. After breakfast, Joe lost consciousness for a minute but came back to me. As he tried to get up using the walker, he fell on his left side and collapsed and was gone, In that instance, I knew he was gone forever.

I called 911, with my heart shattered. My son-in-law, who happens to live nearby, arrived quickly, and we were frantically performing CPR as I prayed to God to bring Joe back. When the medics arrived, they, too, worked on Joe for 49 minutes until they called the time of his death.

Oh. My. God.

"Please, God!" I cried. *"Do not take the love of my life from me!"*

This is not happening... I want you back with me...Life is not fair...

Being a therapist and a life coach for more than 30 years, as well as having cared for most of my family members as they reached the end of their life, I thought I knew what shock and grief was all about. Yet nothing could have prepared me for the storm I now faced. Nothing!

"It is just not fair," I cried, even though I know many things in life are not fair.

I've always said that the challenges we face in life are there to help us grow and to help us get to the other side. Life is filled with adversities of all kinds. Joe and I had experienced our share of challenges together.

This was different.

Despair and fear set in.

I had to face this enormous, heart-wrenching grief, which was made worse by the fact that I also found myself awash in financial distress. The stress of everything at once felt like life had thrown me upside down, and I had landed on my head. I was disoriented. I felt lost.

My daughter Jill and I took on the financial and business responsibilities, as we both wanted to continue Joe's legacy in the mortgage business. A business that is totally different from my life coaching and seminar business, but I did what I had to do. Jill took the lead in heading up the business, putting her all into it while being a mom of twin four-year-olds.

I was in mourning, wearing so many different hats, trying to piece my life together while holding on emotionally and financially. The stress and trauma were overwhelming.

I kept telling myself to go one step at a time.

Fortunately, what I call caring collaboration was in play. So many close family members were there to love and support me. My daughter Dava and her husband were there for me and calmed me down when I was not thinking clearly. They helped me figure things out. What I needed to do in life at this moment and in the business, as did our long-time friend and supporter Crystal, who is the bookkeeper for our mortgage company. My children are a constant ray of support for me. Kit, a friend who worked closely with my husband, offered his care and guidance, making sure we could continue building the business.

I could not have gotten through without my family members, Joe's brothers, and dear friends, who are like extended family, who also helped me get through—texting, calling, and visiting. I thank God for all of their support.

Some tried giving me advice way too early in my initial grieving process. Although caring and well-meaning, it created more anxiety for me. I know my friends and family just wanted me to be "ok." Some were uncomfortable with my grief. For some, it triggers their own grief.

Timing is everything, and I needed time to GRIEVE. I have become intimately familiar with the feeling of being lost, of not being able to breathe with the fear and the ever-present dark hole waiting to consume me.

I thank God for all the prayers and support my family received.

One thing that helped is that I did something I rarely do: I allowed myself to be cared for. I'm a natural caretaker for my grandkids, children, older relatives, friends, and of course, my clients. Given that I was so used to being in that role, letting my guard down and admitting I needed help was big for me. Though I have often coached others to allow support in. It has been tougher for me to do it myself. At times I have found myself isolating and going under, hiding in the darkness, but not for long. I know how important it is to let others in. It is a two-sided gift, and oh so healing when family and friends reach out, check in, and want to be with me. It is a precious time when we are allowed to just be in the moment with one another.

Accepting this support does not make me feel weak or vulnerable. Each person's caring, and support created a light for me to hold on to.

Of course, between the light times, there have been some dark times. Joe and I were a powerful duo. I'd even say that together, we felt invincible, even though we understood how fragile life is. Both of us had a focus and intention to make a difference in the world, one person at a time.

We also made a difference for each other, creating such a magical and romantic love in our almost six decades together from the time we met. We watched our family grow, adding a son-in-law, Brett, and three grandchildren. All of us loved spending time together in the home that Joe and I built on a reservoir. Joe and I loved the simple pleasures of watching the bald eagles fly above us while kayaking or hiking together. We shared many family trips together and loved to experience new places through our travels. Each new adventure brought such joy.

We had a good life.

Joe was a strong, loving, caring man. He made a difference in so many lives that he touched, guiding so many through the steps necessary to stop renting and become proud homeowners. So many of his clients thought owning a home was impossible until they met Joe.

Someone asked me, *"What do you do when Superman dies?"*

He loved to help people, and I was his biggest fan as he was mine.

We worked together to host seminars I designed and facilitated to help people create the transformation they wanted. He was the loving sound man, handling the music during our one- and two-day workshops. There were times that the seminars became a family collaboration, with our daughters taking the time to assist during the seminars and be there for me and the participants. Over time, it felt as if the work I did became a family project, and they helped ensure everything ran smoothly.

Joe was my biggest supporter, forever proud of the difference the seminars made in people's lives.

In fact, he was the one who suggested I create a men's seminar to complement the other retreats we put together. I listened to Joe and created a two-day men's program. It was highly successful and is another part of Joe's legacy that lives on.

He was a blessing to so many, but especially to me and to our family.

We created a life path that wasn't filled with despair, even though we had experienced many of life's traumas along the way. Losing parents, siblings, and other loved ones before their time, financial highs and lows, we never succumbed to despair.

Our motto was and is: be kind and make a difference in someone's life every day, with a smile, a counseling session, or a seminar. Or just giving someone the special gift of truly listening and being present with them.

We believed in and created hope—a glimpse of the light at the end of the tunnel. And at the end of the tunnel was real transformation. We understood that anything is possible if you truly want it—and can believe in yourself.

Unfortunately, there is no manual on grieving, though I do keep in mind the teachings of psychiatrist Elizabeth Kubler-Ross. I had studied briefly with the great Elisabeth, who came up with the five stages of grief: Denial, Anger Bargaining, Depression, and Acceptance.

I am discovering that each phase takes time. It can be difficult to take the necessary steps forward while dealing with prior commitments, keeping busy—maybe too busy—and trying to live the best life I can under the circumstances. Sometimes, I get triggered and feel like I'm all the way back to when I first lost him.

With such a great loss, grief is always there, my broken heart hurting and despair lurking.

One of the things that hurt most is the longing for Joe's physical being.

I feel his presence around me spiritually. I keep hoping I will see him or hear his voice. Yet, when I let myself, I can still feel his presence around me. I find myself having many conversations with him. I hear his deep voice guiding me with a problem I am having. I have also seen things that are hard to explain rationally—like a huge red-tailed hawk on a branch outside my window, looking into my eyes for minutes at a time. The Indians believed that they were messengers from beyond or flashes of green light orbs, especially when face-timing my daughters and grandkids. *"Joe?"* I ask, *"Is that you?"*

Then there are the many dreams I have about our life: when we first met when I was 15 and Joe was 17. I was a swim instructor and counselor at a YWCA camp in Somers, Connecticut. My friend who taught archery became ill, and they called me from teaching swimming and diving to go teach archery. I had no clue how to shoot a bow and arrow, and the head of the camp said, *"They are six to eight-year-olds; how hard can it be?"* They gave me a quick lesson and sent me off to the athletic field, where I shot an arrow into the air and then heard a male voice screaming, *"Did you see that she almost shot me!"* Little did I know Joe and his friend were in the trees looking at the girls in their bathing suits. That was the first time Joe saw me. Back then, he was able to walk into the camp and ask who I was, and they told him. I did not know that we had a mutual friend, and when he told her my name, she said she knew me. He asked her to arrange for me to be at an interfaith youth dance. I remember noticing him standing at the doorway, intensely staring at me until he finally asked me to dance. I dream of that first dance as I was trembling in his arms at such a young age, feeling the passion and how safe I felt at the same time in his arms. I dream of us on our honeymoon, our long talks, and just the way we loved one another. I dream of the way he looked at me with such love.

The dreams that I have are about our life. Sometimes, I wake up with embedded positive messages. Sometimes, he guides me with suggestions about the next steps and that all will be okay. *"Is that you, Joe?"* I wonder and always will.

I know he sees my inner struggle and my inner strength, and I know he does not want me to be in pain. And I know that one day, I will experience joy again. But it will be different.

My niece Nikki sent me a banner that says, *"Life runs in cycles."* The wheel never stops turning. No matter how dark the night, morning comes. No matter how cold the winter, spring comes. I hung her banner in my kitchen, where I can look at it every day.

When you feel despair, know that the wheel is turning. Joy will come. I am grateful for Nikki and all of my nieces for their love and support.

You heal one second, one minute, one day at a time. Healing takes time. One of the most difficult things is knowing that I could not have stopped this from happening. I could not save him. I tell myself that Joe Is now with family members who we both loved, and I feel his joy being with them again.

I know he sees my inner struggle and my inner strength.

"What choice do I have?" I say to myself through the tears. I am doing the best that I can. One minute at a time—one step at a time—I have to keep going as life keeps going.

I push through, surrounding myself with people who care and love me.

Through my work, I have often coached others to let support in. At times, I've found myself isolating, going under, and hiding in the darkness. But not for long. I know how important it is to let others support me.

I feel grace when my daughters and grandchildren put a smile on my face. And then, one of them asks, *"Why did Poppa have to die? Can he come back?"* How do you explain this to three-and-a-half-year-olds or to our 12-year-old grandson?

They see my tears and sadness when they innocently ask these questions. They also miss him very much!

The hole in our lives is palpable. But so is the love that we had. I need to remind myself how blessed I am to have had Joe in my life since we were kids. Even in the throes of grief, I am grateful for experiencing the love of a lifetime. OMG. I so want that back, and always will.

I find myself crying when I need to, and that is okay. I am not able to listen to love songs without crying. And that is also okay.

Enjoying the support of family and friends is okay. No need for guilt for feeling joy with my grandchildren and daughters and friends.

Being able to say "no" to more commitments is also okay. I find that boundaries can get fuzzy while grieving. I have to remind myself to go inside to realign myself, and my priorities are so good for me. Something I teach in my seminars, I also find solace in listening to the meditations I had recorded early in my career!

I found out just how well they work while recording the meditations. I watched as the engineer recording them kept falling asleep! Each minute was costing us money, I would have to stop, get out of the sound booth, and knock at the window to wake him up. He would say, "Wow, they really work. I was skeptical." I find that funny.

Later, Joe and I wanted to listen to the meditations and try them out, and we inevitably fell asleep. We woke up laughing that my voice was able to put us to sleep. I liked to joke with Joe that I was either very good or very boring, being able to put myself to sleep.

These days, whenever I need to listen to my healing meditations, which are now streaming on the internet, I think how proud Joe would be to know that my words and soothing background sounds are on Spotify, iTunes, Pandora, and Amazon Music for others to listen to and that they are out there in the universe helping others heal.

I am now able to listen to some music, which at first I could not do at all. Music has always been a big part of my life, and I find joy and healing while listening. I am doing my best to find time for joy and healing. I take long walks in nature, going inside, balancing myself in the moment.

These moments of self-care are necessary as I am keeping the commitments I had made before Joe's death and now after. It can be challenging to keep doing my work, seeing clients, going to conferences, and doing public speaking. However, I want to move forward even when moving feels so tiring, like walking with heavy boots in wet sand one step at a time. It is also healing and fulfilling to keep promises made.

I decided to go back to my practice. I find supporting others in their lives is helping me heal. Being a facilitator in workshops and a life coach and facilitator is a gift that I have been given by a higher power. This is where I am in my element. Where I know I make a difference. This is so important as I travel along this new life path I find myself on.

Ever since I was a child, I knew instinctively that I wanted to make a difference in other people's lives. I know I was guided to do the work that I am doing. To be vulnerable enough to be the skilled door opener, making it easier for others to walk through the doorway and discover that they can heal. They can create healthier relationships with themselves and others. They can achieve the positive results they want in their lives.

Between all of the personal work I have done with others, my seminar work, and my education and experiences, I feel divinely guided to continue on this path.

Although difficult, I have to talk to myself. I am blessed to be able to live in our sanctuary on a reservoir surrounded by God's grace—eagles, herons, the beavers creating dams, the beautiful water landscape we both enjoyed so much, the huge trees that line the water, the sound of birds everywhere.

I find it helpful to focus on the beautiful, loving family members and dear friends who are in my life.

Despite my grief and loneliness, I let all of this wash over me in gratitude and, of course, also, sadness. And I wish Joe was here to enjoy all of it with me.

I may have lost my husband, but I have not lost my spiritual and inner beliefs that guide me. I know how powerful the words that I speak are and that they create my present reality from moment to moment.

I know that when my emotions are out of extreme balance, my physical body is weakened, as I am very sensitive. I overcame Lupus years ago. For that triumph, I thank God and my belief system. And the ability to live what I teach through neuro-linguistic tools and affirmations. My beliefs and the practice of neuro-linguistic programming (NLP), which is using all of your modalities to send different messages from the brain to the body through the autonomic system, helped me overcome and heal. NLP helped me heal by training my mind to see a new perspective and know how powerful the words and thoughts that we have can co-create healing on many different levels.

I knew that I would be very vulnerable in this time of grief. When I had acute bronchitis for six weeks, I understood it was prolonged by my inner turmoil, stress, and loss.

I began saying positive statements to myself. I gave myself permission to feel what I needed to feel. I began to write down my feelings, which I am doing in this chapter. My hope is that I can help someone else going through something similar while I help myself through writing.My hope is that I may help someone else out there who is going through a great loss.

I know that my journey is a long one. As I travel and learn and grow, I actually smile in between the tears. My gratitude is there for those who reach out and touch me, and I can let the love in.

I am reaching out more often, not always, but getting better. I need support and love, and I am receiving it from those who care and love me.

That is a blessing.

I will experience joy again. I know it. But not in the same way.

The biggest part of living is to acknowledge every moment as it happens. To allow oneself to experience the highs and lows, the heartaches, the raw emotions of sadness, of despair. All while being able to receive the love and support and camaraderie that is all around, to allow all of it to become part of the healing process. To move forward, I choose truth, faith, inner strength, and resiliency. I am living my life as optimally as I can, one step at a time.

I am allowing myself to experience my life in the present moment, looking toward the next steps in my life while allowing both grace and gratitude for what was and will be in my life. I am in the process of redefining the reality of my path and who I am in this world—looking ahead but not too far. On the reservoir, spring is here, and with it, hope and renewal.

Integration

- Are there times that you stop yourself from grieving?
- How could you support and care for yourself more?
- Do you have a circle of support? Who are your go-to people? Do you reach out for support when you need it? If you do not have a circle of support it is time to create one.
- How can you allow yourself to experience the present moment just a little more?

About Gail

"Be kind and make a difference in someone's life every day."

Gail Petrowsky is a transformational life coach who has been leading retreats and private sessions for 30 years, helping individuals and couples heal and go through transitions. She has an MSW, is a certified NLP Master Practioner, and studied at the Albert Ellis Institute for Rational Emotive Behavior Therapy. Gail is a certified Ericksonian therapist, co-author of *A Woman's Book,* and is a creator of healing meditations.

Connect with Gail:
Email: gail@gailpetrowsky.com
www.Gailpetrowsky.com

Chapter 7

The Courage to Be

Meghan Clemens Schelzi

You know those moments, the ones that are equal parts excitement and "I can't believe I'm actually doing this?"

Looking back, those close-my-eyes-cross-my-fingers-and-smile moments have been the guideposts that only now, in reverse, can I see their magnitude. Those moments lead to the most growth, and the most fulfillment and ultimately have evidenced the biggest clarity to me that I am living an aligned life on the path I'm meant to be on.

While at the end of the day, the joy brought forth by these moments outweighs the angst along the way—to say choosing the moments of joy was easy would be just plain false.

As I look back at each choice, each decision, and each moment of growth, there's one quality I notice that is evident in all of them: courage.

But me? Courageous?

Until more recently, that word was not always one that would roll off my tongue when I described myself.

Thoughtful, passionate, creative, committed—those words would arise over and over in Instagram posts, journal entries, emails, etc.

But courage?

Courage takes being brave.

Courage takes detaching from the outcome.

Courage takes trust.

Courage takes believing that even if it doesn't go the way you'd planned—courage is a deep knowing that you will figure it out.

Choosing to be courageous and building up that courage muscle has allowed me to uncover the next right step after the next right step along my journey, which has ultimately led me to live my optimal life.

Who am I? Whose am I? Who am I called to be?

The words were painted in the foyer of the hallway of my dorm during my sophomore year of college.

Every morning on my way out and every evening on my way in, these words repeated in my head.

Nineteen-year-old me had no clue the impact these six words would have on me as they continued to repeat in my mind and shape my life over the next 15 years.

Whether I knew it or not, *Who am I called to be* became the mantra I would build my life around.

It became the voice in my head whenever a big decision loomed—one such moment occurred in the spring of 2020.

March of 2020, to be exact.

As I'm sure many of you can relate to—that March was a major line-in-the-sand moment that changed the course of my life forever.

The previous summer, in August of 2019, after a decade in the elementary classroom, I decided to leave classroom teaching.

Thirty-one-year-old me was naive to think I could always come back!

Thirty-one-year-old me was also brave enough—courageous enough—to trust that the impact that I was put on this planet to create in the world extended far beyond the four walls of my 2nd-grade classroom.

Who am I called to be? pulsed in my mind, stretching me, my thinking, and my vision for the life I was creating.

I began my teaching career in secondary education. After a few short months teaching high school English as a 22-year-old to a classroom full of 18-year-olds, it rapidly became clear that high school English was not meant for me! And although my "don't give up" and "don't quit" attitude attempted to keep me stuck in that career, the voice in my head reminded me to choose growth. To choose alignment. *Who am I called to be,* ran through my mind and gave me the courage to shift and choose my next right step toward an aligned path of working in early childhood education.

When the four walls of a 2nd-grade classroom felt limiting, *Who am I called to be,* gave me the courage to shift and grow again.

Who am I called to be? These were the words on my heart as I chose to leave the classroom, not knowing what was next but trusting my inner knowing that it was clear that there was something else out there—just waiting. It was August 2019, and I had no idea what the world had in store for the next few months, but...

My gut said, "Go!"

My heart said, "Have courage!"

And my brain reminded me to reflect on *Who am I called to be?*

I hit pause.

Packed up my classroom.

Took a breath.

And when a global pandemic shut down the world, *Who am I called to be?* urged me to say "YES" to where I was being called.

I went on to build and grow Next Step Education, a tutoring business, supporting children's learning nationwide and ultimately keeping the JOY in learning for 100s of families and dozens of tutors that joined my mission in the years that followed.

As I write this, Next Step Education is celebrating its fourth summer.

A "little idea" to support a few previous students during the remote learning years grew and grew and grew!

And by the time this book is published and in your hands, I will have opened an in-person tutoring center to carry out our mission!

Beyond my wildest dreams!

Four years of helping children feel confident and proud of who they are and how they show up in the classroom and, more importantly, in the world.

Shifting from teacher to entrepreneur has allowed me the ability to live MY optimal life more fully.

A life lived in continual pursuit of feeling alive.

Feeling present.

An optimal life is lived when you commit to choosing happiness in THIS moment.

Choosing what makes you feel joy and alive today.

An optimal life is built from flow and flexibility, action and adaptability, routine and reinvention.

A continual process of letting go and choosing what to try on next—

Resilient. Forward. Progress.

Taking time to reflect in the moments of fulfillment, feeling the joy, and remembering the growth it took us to get there.

Optimal is what works NOW.

Optimal is what feels good TODAY.

During my years working in classrooms, I knew little about the world of personal development.

It wasn't until I fully stepped out of the classroom that I fully stepped into personal development, self-discovery, coaching, or whatever you choose to call it. Stepping onto that path has changed everything.

I gained the tools I never knew existed—I learned strategies that worked! For myself, for how I impacted children's lives, for how I collaborated with others, for what I believed was possible for my life. Investing in myself in this way has helped me create, expand, and impact others to a greater degree.

Part of the magic I bring to the world is seeing what's missing in a situation and then creating it and going on to share it with others. I always thought if there was no map, no blueprint, no chapter on the "how," then it was one of two things:

1. Wrong

2. Impossible

And more and more, I'm learning that if there's no map, then it means you get to create it. You get to dream it up! You get to make it exactly as you want it to be. And the more you build up that possibility muscle, the more exciting your life gets to be!

Seeing what's *missing* has shifted to seeing what's *possible*—possibility for others—possibility for myself.

Letting go of feeling like I have to choose between two things and instead realizing both can co-exist has allowed my life to continue to grow and expand.

My entrepreneurial dreams began as a business to support children's learning, and it has continued to expand to support teachers.

In the fall of 2022, I developed *Teachers Inspire Teachers* as a community for connection and conversation among teachers. From casual local meet-ups to online mindset workshops and coaching, *Teachers Inspire Teachers* was born out of a desire to build community. I've come to learn that when I don't find a community of people that fit what I'm looking for, it's an opportunity to create it!

I quickly realized that this ability to build and create community was one of the ingredients for MY optimal life! I see how much possibility exists to create a community within the world of education, not only for kids to feel supported but for teachers as well.

I help teachers hold the vision for their optimal life. I help teachers increase their impact and expand their teaching to make their dreams a reality. Whether it's being a more present teacher in their classroom or building a business of their own.

I created *Teachers Inspire Teachers* to support the version of me that existed five, or ten years ago. The me that was looking for community—looking for connection, looking for like-minded people to have conversations with that would help me see my own possibility. A possibility that continues to grow and expand with each next step.

So how do you know when you've found IT? How do you know when you're living an optimal life?

Simply put, you feel it. No boxes to check, no tests to prove, and no approval to seek.

An optimal life is lived when you put your head on the pillow at night and feel in your soul that you are proud of how you showed up in the world that day.

An optimal life is when you wake up in the morning and believe you have the courage within yourself to choose to make yourself proud all over again the next day.

Living each day pointed in the direction of possibility!

So now, it's your turn.

Like I tell the kids: "I do, we do, you do."

Choose the parts of my story that inspire you. Use those to build your own foundation. Take what resonates with you, and leave the rest!

I never expected a global pandemic to shift, shake up, and serve as the foundation for my optimal life, but during the strangest of times, it did just that. It woke me up.

I'm grateful to have experienced such a shift that allowed me to see myself as the leader I get to be in the world of education. I'm grateful to use my story to inspire others' journeys.

I'm grateful to take the last 2500 words to pause, reflect, and re-align myself and my values to my own journey, so that to-morrow I can wake up, continuing to build, grow, and live out my optimal life.

I will leave you with this: *Go be great! The world needs YOU!*

Integration

- What's your big-picture vision for your life? What's one choice you can make today to get you one step closer to your dream life?
- How do you define courage? Write down three moments in your life when you did something that took courage. What inspired you to take that step? How did you feel before, during, and after that choice?
- What's one dream you have always been too afraid to take action on but keep thinking about? What's your "someday" idea? Can you make it happen sooner? Can you take action on it today? What support do you need to make it happen?
- What is one word, phrase, or mantra that serves as your guidepost? What message can you come back to over and over again to help you anchor in and put your feet back on solid ground when you need it?

About Meghan

"Who am I called to be?"

Meghan Clemens Schelzi is a thought leader in education. Meghan holds a BA in English from Fairfield University, an M .Ed in Early Childhood Education from Boston College, Orton Gillingham Trained by the Institute of Multi-Sensory Education, and a 15-year career in Education. In 2020 she founded Next Step Education to support children in building confidence and momentum with their learning, and in 2022, founded *Teachers Inspire Teachers* to build connection, community, and conversation among teachers.

Meghan is a community builder. She believes that community, connection, and conversation are some of the greatest gifts life has to offer. She coaches teachers to create a toolbox of strategies to support them in life beyond the classroom.

Connect with Meghan:
Next Step Education
www.Nextstepeducationtutoring.com
Email: nextstepeducationtutoring@gmail.com
Instagram & Facebook:
@thenextstepeducation
@teachersinspireteachers
@meghanschelzi

Chapter 8

If Not Today, When?

Noelymari Sanchez Velez

We know tomorrow is not promised; we can honor our lives and create one that is full. No, really, we absolutely can!

I've learned the following four important lessons to live an optional life.

Tomorrow is Not Promised

Have you ever woken up and felt like what you experienced the day before was all a dream, perhaps a nightmare?

Then, you come to your senses and realize that what you thought was a dream is, in fact, what you are currently experiencing. Many of us have gone through something like this. Whether it is a trauma, losing a loved one, or a life-altering experience.

This happened to me and my family when we lost our loved one. We never dreamed that we would ever go through such a traumatic event. Losing a loved one can be one of the most devastating experiences we can face, especially when it is unexpected. The pain, the whys, the unanswered questions, and the sadness of not knowing the future potential of that special person.

One of the things that gets me through is knowing I had the chance to love them, to make memories with them, and to find ways always to remember them. This does not take the pain away or the sadness; it just makes it more manageable each day that goes by. My perspective on life has forever changed. I will never take another day for granted, I will live my life to the fullest, I will hug those closest to me a little tighter and look for opportunities to spend more time together. Their light will forever shine in our lives as we continue to heal and find a happier tomorrow.

The concept of time has also changed for me. What was important, what I had been stressing about a few months ago, no longer is. The memories of a particular time have been blocked, and with time, whether I get them back or not is no longer important. I am living for today and what the beautiful future of living a full life will be.

I want to make sure I am living my optimal life every chance I get! Tomorrow is not promised, as things can change in an instant, and I want to make sure that I live my life in a way that honors who I am by living my best life, being healthy, and living a life that is full.

Honoring Your Life

I've had to truly understand who I am and what I am capable of and to love myself fully. Being a woman can be difficult, but being a Latina woman can sometimes make it more difficult or be presented as an obstacle. In our society, we are already being marginalized for being a woman, and sometimes, it feels like you have to prove yourself to be heard. I remember my mom always telling me that I was a born leader, one who took charge when others were trying to figure out what to do. This empowers me to not wait for a solution but to make it happen by taking charge. I make sure I use my voice to speak up about what I believe in and for others who may feel they do not have a voice.

I give you permission to be passionate and fully engaged about what you love to do. Nobody can do what you do better than you. Be an expert at what you do. Bring what you are passionate about to the table without any fears, no matter the obstacles that are put in front of you or the obstacles you think you have.

Honor your life by committing to your passion to rise above any challenges. Make connections with others, be open to new ideas and what others bring to the table. Also, honor your life by knowing when to stop, when to take a break, and smell the flowers. Fill your cup; an empty cup can't satisfy anyone's thirst. Be the example for other women, and be an example for the future generation.

Being Healthy

Take a deeper look at your soul. What is it that you are experiencing that does not make you happy? Is it your health, your weight, or your appearance? All of these may have room for improvement, but remember that you are a beautiful soul with a purpose. Honor who you are and start making the changes you desire, one step at a time.

We may sometimes feel like the whole world is caving in and can't do what we intend or plan to do. During those days, be easy on yourself. Life is so unpredictable, and there are so many unknowns. Take those uncomfortable chances and live your best life.

I remember how I got motivated to stick with my healthy lifestyle finally. All it took was for my doctor to say to lose at least 10 pounds and to see how it goes. I felt that I was being challenged. "*Okay, 10 pounds is not that bad, I can do that, taking baby steps.*" And that is exactly what happened. Starting the journey with a mindset of taking baby steps, making a goal, reaching it, and then putting another goal in place is exactly what has kept me motivated. Don't look at accomplishing your health goals by trying to attack the whole beast; take it one bite at a time, and you will see how graceful you will feel about accomplishing your goals. We do not get there overnight; the journey is incremental.

This could be as simple as taking a walk, trying a new recipe, going to a new coffee shop, traveling to a new town, state, or country, spending more time with those that you love, and simply making others feel your presence and the light you bring.

As we get older, our bodies change; what used to be no longer is. We may no longer be able to be how we used to be. Understand your family history regarding health and any diseases. This will help you understand what you can do for you to live a longer life with your optimal potential.

I know we can't change the hands of time to focus on what we used to be or how we looked before. Today, I am proud to say that I want to work out as much as I can, that I want to run my first half marathon, and that I want to be around to see the newer generation of my family live their lives and be part of their milestones. Every day is a gift, and I intend to be able to uncover those gifts as they come to me.

A Full Life

What do you feel passionate about? What is your why?

I knew in my early 20s that I wanted to work in an environment to make a difference. Through my work in the non-profit world, I've always liked the human connections we make every day, witnessing the changes people make in their lives for the better. It is always so heart-lifting to be able to positively contribute to someone's life when they are in need. In my line of work, I see and know of individuals who have experienced many challenges in their lives. The desperation that you hear in their voice as if there is nowhere else, then turns into a simple thank you by allowing them to have the space to speak and ask. In their time of need, let them borrow your light, your beliefs, and your faith, if necessary, to see that change in them. Making a difference in their lives is why I continue to do what I have done over the years. My contribution to helping them might be small, but I know it has impacted their lives.

By making an impact in someone's life, even when you can't see the final results, you are living a life full of purpose. Always be kind. May your words and actions always be soothing to someone's soul.

Life can change in the blink of an eye. Do what you love, be passionate about it, and do not postpone something you have been wanting to do.

In addition to my non-profit work, working with my husband in our photography business is all about making our clients feel good about themselves, seeing their beauty, and capturing it one frame at a time. This has brought more meaning to my life, to see the beauty in others and to capture their essence during their most memorable moments. Time after time, we have heard our customers say how comfortable they felt in our presence and how we made the experience of photographing them so easy. Honor your presence and others' presence when you work with them and when you share space with them.

Take chances, let your light shine bright, live your life, and honor who you are. Others will adjust.

Integration

- Have you ever had a life-altering experience that changed how you viewed the world forever? If so, what was it? How is your light shining brighter after that experience?
- Have you ever felt you belong or were not being heard? Write about the experience and how it shaped you.
- How can you honor your life and live your passion?
- Write down a few goals to improve your health and well-being.

About Noelymari

"Capturing beauty one frame at a time!"

Noelymari Sanchez Velez works with her husband, Julio, as owners of JCV Freelance Photography, LLC, based out of East Hartford, Connecticut. She is the public relations director and wedding officiant, managing the business with her husband.

Noely also has more than 20 years of experience at an almost 150-year non-profit criminal justice agency based out of Hartford, Connecticut. She is currently the Administrative Manager and IT Liaison, managing projects and IT.

She and her husband engage in a healthy lifestyle by staying active, along with sharing a mutual love for photography and chasing sunsets.

Connect with Noelymari:
Email:jcvfreelancephotography@gmail.com
www.jcv-pics.com
LinkedIn:
https://www.linkedin.com/in/noely-sanchez-velez-1a9758120

Part III

Embodied

Chapter 9

Your Body Is an Oracle

Robin Mayberry

Sandy Moore was draped with pain. A recent surgery had successfully headed off a brain aneurism, but afterward, she was left with the feeling of molten lead being poured over her head and shoulders, leaving her staggering under its weight.

When she came to me, she was there for the pain. I was there for her body. My job was to listen to what it was trying to say so that we could create space for a shift.

Over the course of a few sessions, the pain loosened its hold. As it did, she was freed up to consider the rest of what was true for her. She realized that after years of supporting a partnership as a property manager, she was run ragged. Brain injuries aside, the satisfaction of cleaning and maintaining rental units had run its course. She was spending more and more time wandering in the woods, identifying plants, and filling her pockets with stones.

She was living a straightforward, sensible life, but she was actually a medicine woman. She wanted nothing more than to gather wild herbs on her forest walks and to create tinctures and teas. She wanted to fill her home with crystals and notice the rhythms of the earth, and allow her innate healing energy to flow. She wanted to bloom.

Once she got clear on her truth, she was able to have the necessary conversations about stepping back from the property work so that she could learn herbalism and commune with the forest. Her face relaxed, her shoulders dropped, and her eyes lit up. She became herself.

The work that I do is two-fold. Like Sandy, many of my clients come to me because their bodies get their attention. Frozen shoulders, chronic illness, brutal headaches—that kind of thing. The symptoms are the gateway, but the real magic happens when we start to access the wisdom that's stored behind those symptoms.

My work is to help my clients gently reveal and unwind the patterns, beliefs, and emotional sticking points that gum up the works beneath the surface. Sometimes they come in with physical symptoms, and sometimes it's more subtle—restlessness, anxiety, feeling lost. Either way, their body has gotten their attention.

When our lives become too full, frantic, and overwhelmed to listen to the subtle course-correction cues, our bodies will turn up the volume. They point the compass to a life that's marked by ease, balance, and flow. Our minds might get swamped with expectations and stuck in projects and patterns we know we've outgrown, but our bodies are always ready for the next right step. Like houseplants pointing toward the window, our bodies are always leaning into the light. In other words, our bodies know the way to the optimal life.

An optimal life has three elements: connection, creativity, and flow. We'll start with *connection*, which starts within us and ripples outward. It takes practice to decipher our intuitive messages, but it's a useful skill. Those messages are our flight instruments, pointing the way even when the visibility is poor. If we ignore or miss those signals, we can expect alarms to go off, which, in my line of work, we call symptoms.

The practice of honoring yourself sets you up for honest connection with other humans. We thrive with an array of friends, including the friend you text when you want to be snarky and the friend you call when you want to be soothed. Family, curated.

Good vibes only. Possibly a partner with whom to share your everyday life. Clients, neighbors, co-workers, the barista who knows how to make your coffee.

The optimal life is lush with the energy of community, of give and take, of being there when we're needed, of being seen when we feel all alone in the world. When we hit that balanced note, we feel woven into our own little tribe. We feel safe and secure. We contribute, and we receive in a flow that's dictated by need and circumstance, and when all goes well, there's enough for everybody.

Connection also involves feeling connected to the Earth, to your Spirit life, and to the non-human world. Again, I bring in your body. When we've been through trauma (and who hasn't?), it can make us withdraw from the world at large. When we don't feel safe, we can feel like we're either tucked in behind a twelve-foot wall or floating at a distance from our body. Anything to not go through that whatever-it-was again. As we go through the journey of healing our damage, our capacity for re-connection emerges. We open back up to the smell of cottonwood in May. The suck and hiss of sand at the edge of the ocean. The way robins bob three times before they snap up a worm and the persistence of tree roots nudging up sidewalks. This world is so much and so beautiful. And we belong here.

Then there's *creativity.* Whether you're writing a novel, making a stew, or singing in the shower, you're creating. You're applying your entirely unique thumbprint to the harmonic web of life, and nothing can remain unaffected. Those tomatoes you planted? They change everything.

We're all creative—it's baked into being human—but not all of us know it or allow for it. Part of that is cultural gatekeeping, which wants to make some forms of creativity more valuable than others, using creative shaming to make some work more special—and therefore, more lucrative. This practice is widespread, but it's a lie. There is no creativity that's better. There's only the capacity we all have to engage with our environment using our skills and perspective.

When our life is working well, a well of creative energy is available to us. It's not just the energy to paint landscapes. It's the energy of play: making sidewalk chalk drawings with the kids, goofing around with your keyboard piano. It's the capacity to problem-solve and think a thing through from multiple angles. It's inspired ideas. It can express itself in pinch pots, clog dancing, or a great pot of stew. When we're living optimally, this energy is available without effort. It's just there like language is there.

When we're connected—to our own knowing, and our community, and the Earth—and we're allowing the creative force to travel along the lines of our life, then we are in *flow*.

And here is where life reaches its highest form. When you're in flow, you have reached the place where synchronicities occur as easily as ordering DoorDash on a Friday night. Having the security of connection and the energy of creativity sets you up for effortless ease.

It goes like this. You get an idea. Maybe you'd like to check out the tide pools at Monterey Bay. Your limited-style brain might point out that you don't have any vacation days left at work, there's a dentist bill to pay off, and it's the rainy season anyway. But not flow! Flow takes that flash of an idea and fills up its gas tank with desire. *Wow, would I ever like to see a starfish right now.* You can imagine standing on the rocks with the ocean booming and the clean salt smell and getting still enough to watch the crabs and snails as they gather their courage and work their way among the anemones. You anticipate the feeling of freedom and gratitude, and then you let go because flow doesn't cling.

The next day, your boss leans over the cubicle to ask if you can present your marketing ideas to that software client. The thing is, it's in only two days. And it's a bit of a trip. To Monterey.

If I hadn't seen this kind of thing happen countless times, I would think it was pure fantasy, but synchronicities like this are how I regularly live my life. Life isn't a bus with marked stops. It's a river with a mind of its own. It has energies that will happily carry you along when you're ready to relax into it—and in my experience, this river is friendly. A bit of a ride sometimes, but when we let that flow take us where it will, we arrive at something more delightful, meaningful, or memorable than anything we could have cooked up on our own.

You can't plan an optimal life. How would you even know what to put on the map?

But you can choose it, one awareness at a time. My coach calls it the *Rabbit Path*. We may not know exactly where we'll land, and the path may wind and loop, but when we're in flow, we can see the next right step. And the next. Not a slogging step: a light, dancing step because flow is fun. And before we know it, we're meeting people who open interesting doors. We're lined up with projects that we've been longing to do. We have opportunities to try things we've been curious about. We're doing the pancake on a zipline without quite knowing how we got there. Flow got you there.

I share these ideas with you from the point of view of a person who's lived a less-than-ideal life and has found my way through to a life that belongs to me.

Like so many of the inhabitants of the Healer archetype, I grew up in painful circumstances that shaped my skills and my purpose. I learned to be keenly aware of body language and tone from living in unsafe circumstances. I developed an appreciation for the natural world by escaping on long walks in the woods. I dove into survival strategies that did, in fact, help me to survive, but from which I had to recover just the same: eating disorders, alcoholism, and obsessive relationships among them. You don't have to tell *me* about anxiety, dysmorphia, or a body that's crying out a hundred ways for support. Right there with you, friend. And that, of course, is the gift.

I know that my purpose is to show up as a healer. I first noticed energy running through my hands as a teenager. I wasn't sure exactly what to make of it, but I sensed it was valuable. In my twenties, I saw that some people made a practice of doing healing work, but I didn't really have myself together enough to be valuable to others until my mid-thirties. It takes what it takes. Once I turned the corner into making daily use of my natural skills of running energy and reading bodies, the adventure was launched.

Divine intervention met me at every step of my *Rabbit Path* and has shown me, again and again, how to connect with my own knowing, act on my creative impulses, and find the flow, until I closed the door on self-destruct mode and moved into the state of ease, abundance, and gratitude in which I now get to live. I didn't earn this kind of help. It was grace.

Now I get to offer my own version of the same grace to others and witness their miracles. Like Sandy, who just started her website to list her herbal products. Like Valerie, whose immovable shoulder resolved after she cleared up old business with her ex. Like Carissa, who got the feeling back in her hands when she acknowledged she was burned out with hands-on bodywork and instead was ready to write a novel. By having the courage to explore their inner messages, each of them expanded the gorgeousness of their life—*and* repaired their bodies.

The optimal life isn't hidden. It isn't mysterious. It's available to us all the time, not by achieving, striving, succeeding, or amassing, but by dropping into our own knowing. It's the connected life: to our own guidance, to the planet, to our tribe. It's the creative life: taking chances with making the ideas that come to you into something real. It's a life in flow, trusting the river.

The optimal life is a healed life. When we live it, we ripple the healing outward until one day, maybe soon, all those ripples overlap, and we all, all at once, remember who we are.

Integration

- How does your body send you messages? (Intuition, sensation, symptoms?) Do you tend to listen to those messages?
- Set a timer for five minutes and list everything you can think of that you'd like to make. Anything from a novel to an online class to a great conversation to a choreographed puppet show is fair game. Everything you can think of! Next, circle three of the most interesting things you wrote down. What's in the way of creating them?
- How do you know when you're in Flow?

About Robin

"You can't plan an optimal life. But you can choose it, one awareness at a time."

Robin Mayberry transformed her own decades-long dysmorphia, eating disorders, and substance abuse by gently restoring her relationship with her body. She now uses her superpowers as a Reflector, clairsentient, transformational coach, and BodyTalk™ practitioner to help you discover and process the messages that arise through the oracle of your own body. The result is an abundant life in an easy body, in flow with a Universe that can't wait to see what you do next.

Connect with Robin:
Email: robin@robinmayberry.com

Chapter 10

I Am Love

Jacquelyn Santiago Nazario

I worked non-stop during the summer of 1994, and I walked every day from the North end of Lawrence to the South end, where I lived in the stadium housing projects. A week after meeting him, we started dating. He had picked me up from work and dropped me off at my aunt's house every day, saving me an hour's walk home. He bought me small gifts to express his interest and appreciation. A kiss on the railroad tracks launched our relationship. He made me feel like I was worthy of love.

Finally, three months after meeting, I could not stop thinking about him. At 17 years old, the allure of a man three years older was intense. I would skip school to go into the housing projects to see him. The desire and longing for connection and intimacy kept me pushing boundaries in all aspects of my life.

I had finally found the man who thought I was beautiful and sexy. I did not care that my parents disliked him. He told me that he loved me, so there was nothing I would not do for him. I proved my love for him by remaining loyal when he went to jail for a year—sending him money and inspirational letters and remaining faithful. Six months after he came home, I decided to skip school again and surprise him at his new apartment that he shared with a couple of friends and his sibling. They told me that he was at a different house; from the look on their faces, I could tell that something was terribly wrong. I overheard his friend say my boyfriend "was caught now," and I realized that he was cheating while he thought I was attending school.

I arrived at the house my boyfriend was visiting. I searched for a way to break into the first floor. I was frantic to know what he was doing at this house and who was with him. When I could not find a way into the high windows, I knocked on the door with fierce intensity. The female who answered the door pretended not to know who I was looking for. I described him and told her who I was.

After a few minutes of talking, I could tell her face transformed from rigid and angry to one of compassion. This was her apartment, and she did not want any problems. She felt he was not an honest man. Then confirmed that he had been dating her cousin, who was well aware that he had a girlfriend. She says, *"They left out the back door as we talked; I gave them the chance to escape."*

I ran down the street as hard as I could and yelled profanities at them. My heart wanted to pulse out of my mouth. My words were fiery. I felt like I screamed with all the energy in my body, but the words belly-flopped off my lips. I was too far.

I came to an abrupt halt as I approached the locked door to a brick apartment building where they sought refuge. As I panted outside the door, I started to become aware of my surroundings. I was in a poor section of Lawrence known for assaults, drug dealing, and prostitution. It was not safe, but more importantly, I felt stupid, defeated, betrayed, inferior, and worthless again. I berated myself as I walked an hour home. How stupid and foolish I had been to believe that someone could love me.

I reminded myself that I would always be the worthless little six-year-old girl. Instantly relived my rape in detail, felt the filth on my body, and the feeling of helplessness washed over my body again. It was my fate to be used and discarded due to my past. God now knew that I was even less pure and no one would love me again. Yet, I called him at home the next night and told him that I forgave him and we could work it out. People make mistakes.

My mother saw my depression and anxiety rising. She was also vigilant to make sure I did not set a decision into motion that I could regret for my entire life. I had already had a sheriff come to my parent's house. I had mailed an illegal object to my boyfriend in jail. It was a crucifix as I hoped that God would deliver him from the drug charges he was facing. She was furious as I brought another shame by linking my family to illicit acts. I think her greatest fear was that I would become pregnant to keep our love alive.

She kept me busy with home, work, and school and grounded me for a couple of weeks. These couple of weeks were different from the normal physical punishment. She talked to me like a young woman. Sharing stories about herself as a young girl, warning me that women withstand the worst of the responsibilities when it comes to homemaking.

She also encouraged me, saying in two more weeks, you will be the first in our family to attend college. She dreamed of her daughter becoming a "professional." She never gave me a specific profession, though. I wondered if she just could not imagine the wide variety of professions available to her daughter. I recognize now that I hid so many parts of me that I did not let anyone know who I truly was. I believe that I had no idea who I was truly. I was too busy hiding the shadows of a girl who felt unlovable, unworthy, and not enough.

I found a few more trauma-filled relationships. When I committed to relationships, I often said *yes* when I really wanted to say *no*. I did not uphold boundaries because I was fearful of losing the love. I had a deep fear of abandonment and, throughout the process, started immersing myself deeper and deeper into my partner's desires to the point I lost myself. I never asked myself what I needed. In fact, I did not believe I mattered. I did not miss an opportunity to degrade myself. Perhaps I was subconsciously battering myself with words so it would hurt less when others betrayed or injured me. I did not want to trust any man enough to allow him to violate me in any way again.

I went to massage school, where I discovered the mind, body, and spirit connection. The first massage I received at massage school was from a gifted spiritual instructor. She focused on my hip flexors, and I began to cry quietly into the blanket under which I was hiding my face. She later informed me that this kind of emotional release happens with people who hold sexual abuse trauma and feelings of unworthiness in their pelvic area. She wanted to apologize if this was not the case for me. She also told me that if the circumstances were, in fact, true, I should get help to dig deeper into the hurt. Initially, I thought she was crazy; who purposely seeks to hurt and talk about it? Eventually, I sought therapy to address the source of my pain. Years later, I worked with a spiritual coach to complement my clinical therapy.

Over the years, I realized that there were key lessons that led to my transformation. I focused on one small goal at a time. I started my journey by addressing negative self-talk. My rape as a six-year-old and then the infidelity of men I trusted eroded my self-confidence and caused depression and anxiety. The depression and anxiety manifested itself in negative self-talk. I punished myself with an inner dialogue that suppressed my belief in my potential. I created a deep three-step plan to defeat the negative self-talk and spirit of insecurity that came from so much pain. Awareness, Confronting Negativity, and Challenge.

Awareness: *I am not happy with who I am.* I told myself that I should be anyone except myself. I wanted to be Irene Cara Escalera and do a flash dance to her 80s song, "What a Feeling." She seemed free and confident. In reality, I would like to be anyone who was not as damaged as I was.

I abused myself daily by insulting all of my physical features. The more negativity I fed myself, the more toxic my behaviors and thinking became. I realized later in life that I was speaking death into my mind and spirit every time I disparaged myself. The pressure of the pain was unbearable, and I blamed everyone for my circumstances until my spiritual coach asked me to explore and fall in love with myself.

What kinds of things made me happy? What did others love about me? What do I need to let go of? Do I love my uniqueness? What dragged my spirit down? The exploration journey allowed me to accept these pieces of me and find the love I needed to start my transformation.

I started to intentionally notice the negativity surrounding my poor self-esteem and started the brave journey of confronting them.

Confronting My Negativity: *Bad things always happen to me because that is the story of my life.*

Another common negative self-talk phrase that I had on repeat. I told myself that I should not expect anything else because good things never really last. I should be happy with what I have because other people have it worse. I told myself so many narratives to keep myself in the cycle of low expectations.

Then, I realized that I had the power to change my future once I could change the way I thought about myself. This meant that I had to follow my emotions to the root. The journey allowed me to feel the pain and examine the origin of that pain instead of making myself busy with relationships. As long as I was busy and running away from the pain, I could not grow and thrive.

I started to love my heart, value my thoughts, and believe in my physical beauty. I learned which activities made me happy. Most importantly, I began to appreciate my whole self: body, mind, and spirit. I stopped hiding my past, living in shame, and became comfortable with the fact that I could never be perfect, no matter how hard I tried. I realized that I suffered, but that turmoil could not be the crutch I used to cater to my trauma. I had the ability to decrease the pain if I could stop blaming others for my current condition.

Whenever a situation triggered a negative thought, caused anger, or other powerful emotions, I stopped to ask why this had happened and what I could learn about myself. I realized that while I could not change some situations, I could change my reaction to the circumstances. I could force myself to confront the hurt I was feeling.

I asked myself key questions about my negative thoughts and self-talk:

1. Is this thought true? Or is my trauma causing me to blame myself as a form of self-punishment?

I further investigated the validity of my thoughts by filtering through the following:

- Catastrophizing: Is my brain jumping to the worst possible conclusion about myself?
- Polarization: Is my brain only considering extreme circumstances without considering the facts?
- Overgeneralization: Is my brain jumping to false conclusions with limited information or flawed data?
- Comparison: Did my brain unfairly compare myself to others?

2. If the thought is true, how can I work to change this reality if it negatively affects my well-being and inhibits my growth?

Challenging myself: Confronting my negative self-talk revealed that most of my thoughts were untrue, and I needed to reframe my thoughts. Challenge myself to change the old programming that circulated through the synapses in my brain and, instead, create new pathways filled with hope and affirmations. Speaking with positivity allowed me to change the energy around the old programming. I started to speak life into myself and declare to the universe that I rejected the lies of the past and felt worthy of love. Each cell in my body confirmed that I matter and I am enough.

It was difficult to catch myself in the act of wounding myself because it had become so normal. I literally had to catch the thoughts in my mind and words as they left my mouth. Each time I caught myself, I would make myself reframe the negativity into positivity. I would make myself say it aloud. I started to read affirmations daily and journal about gratitude and appreciation of myself.

Every once in a while, I did confront a thought that was true. For example, *I am not a good public speaker.* I learned to reframe this thought and create a goal to overcome the challenge. I changed my talk to declare I am practicing my public speaking so I can grow into becoming an incredible orator. I acquired coaches, watched public speaking and presentation videos, and, most importantly, stepped out of my comfort zone. I accepted speaking engagements for small settings and presented alongside strong presenters to learn from my experiences.

I reminded myself often that this is a learning journey. I showed myself grace through the growth process. I committed to my growth by taking on healthy challenges. In that process, I created a breakthrough from the limiting beliefs that held me back from experiencing freedom, love, and happiness. My brain began to create a new positive and peaceful normal. The new positive thoughts and self-talk activated the feel-good hormones in my body that allowed me to sleep better and decrease anxiety and depression.

These three steps of awareness, confronting negativity, and challenging myself were the beginning phases of a transformation. Once I could control my thoughts, I felt better in my body and mind. Those thoughts and emotions eventually influenced my behaviors because my actions now reflected my values. I consciously learned to treat myself with dignity and respect as well as speak to myself with honor and love. I acknowledge my worthiness and tarnish with grace. Since I love myself, I attract love and have become love.

Integration

When experiencing negative thoughts and self-talk, ask yourself these key questions:

- Is this thought true? Or is my trauma causing me to blame myself as a form of self-punishment?
- Investigate the thought further by filtering it through these questions:
- *Catastrophizing:* Is my brain jumping to the worst possible conclusion about myself?
- *Polarization:* Is my brain only considering extreme circumstances without considering the facts?
- *Overgeneralization:* Is my brain jumping to false conclusions with limited information or flawed data?
- *Comparison:* Did my brain unfairly compare myself to others?
- If the thought is true, how can I work to change this reality if it negatively affects my well-being and inhibits my growth?

About Jacquelyn

Jacquelyn Santiago Nazario is the Chief Executive Officer of COMPASS Youth Collaborative, a Human Relations Commissioner for the City of Hartford, and an author. Jackie is a national violence prevention leader, a youth development advocate, a champion for youth equity, and an activist for youth living in risk. She has affected the lives of thousands of marginalized Brown and Black people in poverty-stricken communities and schools. Jackie is the co-author of *Becoming Her* and has received several awards including the Hartford Business Journal's "40 under 40" award.

Jackie is a loving mother and family is her greatest pride and joy. She is the wife of her adoring and highly accomplished husband Iran Nazario.

Connect with Jackie:
Email: JackieNazarioMotivation@gmail.com
Linked In:
https://www.linkedin.com/in/jacquelyn-santiago-nazario-481 67b125
www.nazariomotivation.com

Chapter 11

Optimizing Your Joy

Mary Ann Pack

"No! We don't do that!"

This was the answer I received so many times during my childhood as I would ask to do something that seemed like fun. I watched other kids doing these things and didn't understand why it wasn't okay for me. It could be something as simple as watching a popular TV show, wanting a new outfit, or even square dancing in gym class (of course, I'm dating myself!).

It's not that my parents were mean or unreasonable; they simply believed every little rule and dogma that the church taught as the gospel truth. And our gospel truth was a very strict and patriarchal system. Women were the reason for original sin and cursed with childbearing pain. I was taught that my needs and wants were not as important as the man in my life. From early on, I was taught that I would be expected to sacrifice what I wanted so that my husband could have what he deemed best. It was a badge of honor to serve until exhausted.

I never really faired well with all the restrictive dogma. I couldn't seem to keep the rules and would always get into trouble. Spankings were common, and my little butterfly spirit was being squashed into conformity through guilt and shame.

Life was an emotional rollercoaster. I could be happy and joyful *only* if I thought I was obeying the rules and being a "good girl." So, joy was very conditional for me.

I took solace in being in nature with my frogs and bugs and rocks and things. I was always making an art project from my treasures found outside. I tended to play alone unless the kids on the street were out. Or if we were playing softball in our backyard with the neighborhood kids. I was a tomboy, and my older identical twin sisters were squeamish around my forms of play.

As a young woman, I didn't make good decisions because I had no practice in making decisions because much of my life was decided for me. When I did get married and had my sons, I was miserable and so depressed I didn't want to live. Yet, I couldn't leave my babies without a mom. So, I sucked it up and trodded on.

Of course, there were moments of happiness and joy. But they were always conditional and fleeting because I could never measure up. *Was I a good submissive wife for my husband and a virtuous, sacrificing mom? Was I doing good by sacrificing my desires for the good of the family? Was my constant illnesses and migraines punishment for my sins? Was I missing the big lesson I was supposed to learn so everything would be rosy?*

My misery finally broke me in my mid-thirties. I sought out natural healing at a health food store. I told the owner to "fix me." That beautiful woman took the time to mentor me back to health in many ways. Studying herbs and supplementation allowed me to study other things like metaphysics, crystals (which I've always loved and didn't know why), energy healing, and so much more!

For another ten years, I studied and started coaching health and wellness. I hadn't yet put it together that much of my illness stemmed from my mindset. Until I found Louise Hay's book, *You Can Heal Your Life*. That book allowed me to see that my emotions were driving my illness because of the toxic beliefs I had held for so long. I didn't realize my body was listening to my complaining and misery and was responding in kind.

Once I began evaluating my beliefs by how they made me feel, I realized I needed to release many of them. I learned that how I feel indicates my true alignment with my inner God-force/Soul/Inner Being. If a belief felt good to my soul, I knew it was MY Truth. Any belief that felt bad was a lie, and I was free to release it.

This process of evaluating my beliefs has served me well over the years. Finding my mentor, Abraham-Hicks, helped me shift my mindset for continued well-being. I shifted my coaching and also began writing my blog. Writing became a healing outlet for me since I had not been allowed to use my voice for so many years.

Now, I adore writing and love expressing my thoughts through writing, podcasting, and helping others tell their stories. My mission is to spread more love and joy in the world, so writing and storytelling seemed a perfect match!

When I came across a quote from Abraham-Hicks a few years ago about us being joy and that joy is our purpose, it shifted everything! I decided to claim the title of Joy Advocate. At first, I felt some angst about what others might think about that, but I did it anyway! I knew if I felt bad worrying what others thought about me claiming that I AM JOY, my Inner Being must really love it and feel good about it!

So, it stuck! I adore helping others share their stories of transformation from trauma into joy. Trauma is not always blatant. Many times, trauma is a subtle indoctrination that steals our joy over many years. So, I believe that we all have some sort of indoctrination that is no longer serving our highest good. Releasing that can sometimes come through writing a chapter in a book like this one or writing your very own book! Sometimes, it's so difficult to tell your story that you need support from a ghostwriter. My ghostwriting system is simply telling me your story as I ask questions. It can feel safer to talk it through than to write it down. I want to encourage and support anyone with a story to tell that ends in joy! I'm always looking for those who align with my mission to spread love, joy, and hope for healing.

In considering what makes for an optimal life, I would have to say that we first have to understand who we really are. If we don't have that foundation, we don't know who we are and will wander aimlessly through life. My spirit guides, *The Many,* told me early on in our conversations to remind everyone of their innate goodness. I know they understand how important it is to believe in our goodness because so many of us were indoctrinated to believe in our unworthiness and shame.

For me, knowing that I am joy embodied, I am love embodied, knowing that I am an extension of the pure positive energy of Source, has been the strongest foundation on which to build an optimal life.

Next, I believe we will only live an optimal life if we deliberately choose our thoughts by how they make us feel. We all want to feel good—that's why we want anything—to feel good. If we believe something that doesn't feel good, then we have the power to change that belief because we are in control of our thoughts. Since beliefs are only thoughts we repeat to ourselves until they become beliefs, we also have the power to shift those beliefs as we shift our focused thought patterns!

It is absolutely imperative to live with an attitude of appreciation. Appreciation is not just a good feeling; it is an energetic state of being. This is an important distinction. Not only are we love and joy embodied, but we are also appreciation embodied! These states of being are the essence of who Source IS—and us, by extension!

If we're living in love, joy, and appreciation, we are living the optimal lives that we intended when we came into this physical realm. This understanding is why I know that I'm meant to write books that support people in knowing who they are and living their optimal lives!

My *We Are Joy* book series begins with a foundational book about understanding who we are as joy. The second book was co-authored with April Goff Brown and supports anyone looking for the best crystals for healing in specific areas of their lives. Book three is a six-month gratitude journal because I know how important it is to be in gratitude and appreciation. Book four was a podcast and book anthology project entitled *Unmuted Voices.* Twelve inspirational authors joined me in sharing their beautiful, empowering stories of overcoming trauma and indoctrination to speak and live their truth.

My most recent book, *My Dream Life Storybook,* is a journal-style book that offers 30 chapters for the reader to write their life stories exactly how they want them to be. I encourage my readers to tell a new story of *their* optimal life, feel the exhilarating emotions attached to that dream life, and then relax, trust, and receive it fully! This book is a true keepsake and can be left as a legacy.

I know how important it is to have practical tools to integrate the transformation we are seeking. That's why all of my books have integrative exercises included in every chapter. **We don't need more knowledge; we need the wisdom that comes from the integration of what we're learning to live our full, optimal lives!**

No matter what you're writing, it is the fastest way to evoke change. If you're writing a sad story, you will evoke more sadness. If, on the other hand, you are writing about your sadness and how you came through it into joy, you will evoke more joy if that is the dominant feeling while writing. If you appreciate all that you went through to honor who you are, in the end, you will come back into the love and joy of who you are because your Inner Being is always calling you and showing you the path to more—more love, more joy, more appreciation, and more life!

In thinking back over the experience of working with the authors in *Unmuted Voices,* I remember one author who was quite surprised at what Source led her to talk about on the podcast. As she told her story of breast cancer and how she decided to show up authentically—in all the good, bad, and ugly of treatment—she saw what a blessing her vulnerability was for others. She works as an inclusion officer for a non-profit and had a side gig as a consultant. Once she participated in the podcast, told her story, and wrote her chapter, it made her realize she had the freedom to go bigger! To live in a bigger way, she created her website to take her consulting work to a wider audience! This unmuting process opened the opportunity for her to live optimally in loving service to others.

If you are feeling that you're not living your optimal life, take heart. You're not alone. Every time I write something, teach something, or give a message to someone asking a question of my spirit guides, *The Many*, I am speaking to myself first! Even though I know this stuff, I need constant reminding.

Life is a journey, and to live optimally, you must enjoy it all along the way. Of course, there will always be ups and downs. That's life. We must have the contrast of what we don't want in order to know what we do want. That's how we make preferences, and that's what keeps the eternalness in eternity! **The mantra of the Universe is MORE—more love, more joy, more creation, more expansion, and more life! You will only be satisfied and fulfilled as you choose MORE of the optimal life you intentionally came to live!**

So, how do we get started on this optimal life path?

Know who you are as joy embodied. You will do this by developing a relationship with your Inner Being. Ask her what she knows, thinks, and feels about who you are. Then listen and take copious notes!

Shift your beliefs by shifting your deliberately chosen thoughts. You are the only one in control of your thoughts. Many times, it can feel that our thoughts control us, but that is not true. I can say this for a fact because when we think we have no control over our thoughts, it feels so disempowering and bad. That feeling indicates it's a lie. As you reach for thoughts that soothe and bring relief, you will know those are aligned with your Inner Being. The better you feel by what you're thinking, the more you can *know* you are aligned with your true Self.

Get into and maintain an attitude of appreciation! Appreciation is the key to everything we want—especially that awesome optimal life we dream about! If you only focused on living with an appreciative attitude, you would live the most fulfilling, meaningful life of abundance and joy. Appreciation is best friends with love, joy, and abundance!

Integration

- If there was no limitation to anything you wanted, tell the story of that optimal life. Write it with feelings of exhilaration, adventure, and appreciation for this dream life as if you're already living it now!
- Make lists of what is going right in your life and feel the appreciation and gratitude deeply. Breathe it in while you write.
- Set alarms on your phone to ding and remind you to stop and notice how you're feeling throughout the day. This will help you get into the habit of awareness and then shift the thought pattern that created any negative emotions. If you're feeling good, keep going! Remember, your emotions tell on your thoughts every single time. Make it a fun game to see how good you can feel every day!

ABOUT MARY ANN

"The mantra of the Universe is MORE—more love, more joy, more creation, more expansion, and more life!"

Mary Ann Pack is a spiritual medium, best-selling author, publisher at Envision Greatness Press, and joy advocate. Her mission is to spread more love and joy in the world by writing, publishing, coaching, and podcasting in support of others as they use their voices for messages of hope and healing.

If you have a book being called through you, want to participate in a collaborative book project, need ghostwriting, or want a customized journal to uplevel an event or program, visit her website to explore publishing. Her published books, including the *We Are Joy!* series, are available on the website. Let's write the world happy, one word at a time!

Connect with Mary Ann:
www.EnvisionGreatness.com
Email: envisiongreatnessllc@gmail.com
https://linktr.ee/maryannpack

PART IV

PURPOSE

CHAPTER 12

FINDING LIFE'S CALLING

LINDA PIOTROWSKI

I was six years old when Muzz, my paternal grandmother, came to stay with us. My mother was caring for her while she recovered from surgery for breast cancer. My vital, fun grandmother was in the bed in our front bedroom, flat on her back, obviously in pain. I loved her. This was the grandmother who taught me to read and bake and helped me learn to sew.

I remember being struck by how frail and weak she seemed. I would keep her company, often just holding her hand. At times, I read her stories until she said she was tired and needed to rest. I'd leave the room, returning only when my mother went to bring her food or to change her bandages. I prided myself on not being afraid to see the bandages or my grandmother's scar where her breast had been. Muzz, of course, encouraged my mother to let me stay. Muzz was not afraid of anything. She taught me to be the same. It was during those weeks of Muzz's recuperation that the seeds were sown for the work that I would eventually train for, embrace, and love.

For a number of years, I worked as a teacher. I then became a religious education director. While I was in seminary getting a master's degree in theological studies, I spent a semester as a chaplain intern in a major metropolitan hospital. It was a rigorous program involving didactics, study, verbatims, and visits with patients of all ages. My assignment was to accompany patients in uncovering the meaning and purpose of their lives and to help them make some sense of the health crises they were experiencing. I tentatively approached my first patient. As I invited him to tell me his story, I discovered that I knew how to engage, be present, listen to the words under the words, reflect back to them what I was hearing, and help. I found it! My life's calling.

I continued to study to qualify as a board-certified chaplain. I worked in nursing homes, hospitals, palliative care, and in homes as a hospice chaplain. The work of a chaplain is far different from most people's impressions of chaplains. Mine was not to convince people to accept God as a way to recover or to begin to practice a certain religion. My work was to help people discover the meaning of their illness. What was this experience teaching them? What was the meaning and purpose of their life? What actions could help them to find wholeness? Did they have a relationship with something "Other?"

Often, what resulted was not physical wellness; rather, it was deep-down soul wellness. By sharing their stories, we could often uncover what could help them to feel whole. Perhaps it was as simple as telling someone, *"I love you."* It might be saying, *"I'm sorry. Please forgive me."* or *"I forgive you for things I hold against you."* It might simply be, *"Thank you."* Often, it included, *"Goodbye."*

Ministering as a chaplain taught me to be tolerant, to accept rejection, to talk less, and to listen more. It taught me to extend kindness and to look past color, gender, creed, and sexual orientation. It taught me to accept each person as unique, a never to be seen again individual.

In learning to listen carefully in order to help each person puzzle out the meaning of their life, I learned to do the same in my own life. I learned to accept others' follies and foibles and be graceful to my own.

Most importantly, I think, in helping others to do this in their lives, I learned to pay attention to my own life. I learned to see the beauty and tragedy each day can hold. I learned to appreciate all of life as the gift it is. I learned to listen to my life.

To me, living an optimal life involves listening to my life and uncovering the richness and beauty within. It means responding to what I uncover by living in a way that truly honors my core values and beliefs. This involves paying attention to my own life and the world around me. It involves learning to appreciate that all of life has the potential to be sacred. The work of finding meaning in life and work involves paying attention to the little things as well as the big things.

While I was working as a chaplain, patients and family members taught me this in so many ways. One patient was a young woman, MaryAnn (not her real name). She was married with three children, a husband, parents, and siblings who loved her. One evening, while decorating a cake for her youngest son's birthday party, she suddenly collapsed to the floor in a seizure. Within minutes, she was unconscious. Arriving by ambulance, she was admitted to our neurological unit. When I arrived in her room, I was greeted by a distraught husband and her parents.

In the days, weeks, and, yes, months to come, she never regained consciousness. Yet, her father and mother came faithfully, over a distance of 65 miles, to sit with her and advocate with her doctors. Her father could sometimes convince his wife to take a day off, but he never missed a day. Together, we learned about each other and the patient. We laughed, cried, wondered, railed against the vagaries of life, and sometimes prayed. MaryAnn was a vital part of these conversations. We were aware of her presence and the possibility that she might be hearing us. Her parents, husband, and I held her hand and included her as we talked.

This family and many like them taught me so many things. One is that life can change in an instant. Most importantly, I learned that love never gives up. It looks like being faithful, being present, and advocating for what someone needs. It means telling the stories, asking forgiveness, noticing the little things, and, when necessary, letting go.

I'm retired from chaplaincy now, yet what I learned as a chaplain continues to inform my life. I wake up each morning aware of the gift of each day. I've learned to live with the little limitations that come with aging. I am grateful for each day—even the bad or painful ones. I've learned to notice things, to keep an account of my days, to embrace beauty, and to hold life as sacred.

I've taken my chaplaincy skills and continued to learn. After completing 100 hours of training, I've been commissioned as a Stephen Minister and a commissioned Stephen Leader, I am available to accompany people through the difficult times of their lives, be it the death of a spouse, loneliness, or attempting to find meaning in their lives. It helps me to live fully, to give to others, and to continue to reflect on my own life.

Living an optimal life, for me, means paying attention to the life I am living now. Regardless of our age, we would do well to ask: What are my core values? Is the life I am living now giving evidence to them?

Pay attention to your life. Be faithful to it in a way that works for you. That might be keeping a journal. Don't know where to start? Ask yourself key questions. Make a list of your answers. Then think about your day. Did your activities reflect your values? Does the work you do assist you in making your values real in the world? What do you need to change in order to have your life reflect your values? What are you grateful for? What are your daily intentions? You get the idea.

Don't give your time to things that are not worthy of you. Set a routine and try your best to stick to it. Living an optimal life doesn't mean that you will be happy all the time. What it does mean is you will be living in concert with your values.

Integration

- Be attentive to your thoughts upon awakening. Try to be sure they include being grateful for another day of life. If possible, do a brief journal entry. Describe one thing you are grateful for. Then, write down at least one thing you want to spend your precious time on. Keep this in mind as a kind of touchstone throughout your day.

- As Socrates wrote: *"An unexamined life is not worth living."* Engage in an evening inventory. Look at how you intended to live this day. Did you succeed? If not, write about what held you back. Look at what you spent your precious time doing. Write about what you notice about how you spent your time. Remember, though, that life's not all about productivity. It is about living your values. Were you able to do that? If not, what held you back? If yes, how can you do more of that? End by writing about at least one thing you noticed that you can be grateful for.

- Life really is a work of art. Ask yourself, what talents, gifts, patience, practice, and dedication do I bring to my life? If all this seems a bit much, write about why it seems like too much.

About Linda

"Ministering as a chaplain taught me to be tolerant, to accept rejection, to talk less, and to listen more."

Linda F. Piotrowski is a retired board-certified chaplain. She is a friend, widow, mother, and grandmother. She holds a Master's degree in Theological Studies from St. Francis Seminary in Milwaukee, Wisconsin, as well as certification as a writing facilitator from the Amherst Writers and Artists in Amherst, Massachusetts. She has completed advanced study in palliative care and being with the dying. She ministered for over 40 years as a chaplain and director of spiritual care. She currently serves as a Stephen Minister for Valley Presbyterian Church in Green Valley, Arizona.

Connect with Linda:
Email: giraffe109@gmail.com

Chapter 13

Speak Your Purpose

Shannon Malkin Daniels

I guess you could say my journey to becoming a public speaking, communication, and confidence coach started at the young age of six. Possessing an overabundance of energy, my parents signed me up for gymnastics. Being that young, I can't really remember if I chose gymnastics or if they chose it for me. What I can remember is being incredibly scared of the uneven bars. More specifically, transitioning from the high bar to the low bar was a jump that seemed tremendous to such a little tike, even at a kid-friendly height. But I was determined to overcome my fear and give it a try, so I stuck with it.

As burgeoning gymnasts, our coach encouraged our parents to enroll us in ballet to help increase our flexibility. Fortunately for my mom and dad, there was a ballet studio inside the gym, so it was one drop-off for two activities—what parent doesn't love that!?

Little did they know that I would fall in love with dance, and gymnastics would quickly become a thing of the past. That was the beginning of my love for dance, which I would continue doing into my late twenties when my knees decided it was time to hang up my dance shoes. Before throwing in the proverbial towel, I danced ballet, jazz, clogging, chorus line, pom, and hip-hop. I was on my middle school and high school dance teams and had the opportunity to compete at state and national competitions (those trips to Disney were fun and exciting!). I even taught dance classes for a while in college.

Looking back, I believe that starting dance at such a young age is what led to my lack of stage fright and comfort being the center of attention. Okay, so maybe my family would say differently, having garnered nicknames from them such as "ham bone," "hammy," and "bopper" before ever stepping foot into a dance studio. But I digress. I truly do believe that my dance experience prepared me for what would ultimately become my passion for speaking and career as a public speaking, communication, and confidence coach.

Weirdly enough, I didn't begin my career there. It was a winding journey—and a lot of 'resisting the call'—that kept me from fulfilling my purpose earlier in life. I originally went to college for aerospace and mechanical engineering. I wanted to design rockets and cars and was especially interested in harnessing thermonuclear fusion as a fuel source that would enable humans to travel deeper into space. I was great at the problem-solving, science, and engineering aspects of the degree, but me and math just didn't get along. You could say it was a hate-hate relationship: I hated doing math problems, and math problems hated being solved by me. Since I couldn't see myself spending a lifetime doing math equations, I changed my major. . . several times.

I knew I loved writing, but journalism was too niche. I thought marketing would be fun because I love being creative, but economics was not my jam. After battle-testing a few more majors but never quite landing on one, an advisor suggested liberal studies. I remember asking, *"Isn't that a joke degree?"* To which he responded that it was actually becoming a more highly sought-after degree because of its versatility. He explained that I could combine all my passions (well, three anyway) into a major to have a wider breadth of knowledge. He also said that employers were seeking out liberal arts majors because they are more well-rounded. Whether that was the truth or just his way to get me to settle on a degree, I'll never know. But what I can tell you is that I finally found my place and my people.

I ended up changing my major to liberal arts with a primary concentration in communications (words and I DID get along) and letters (which was a fancy word for writing), with a minor in marketing. So, I got the marketing, advertising, writing, and journalism all rolled into one, and I loved every minute of it. What I didn't expect were the aspects of communications that I both loved and excelled at—interpersonal and public speaking. In fact, I loved interpersonal so much that I decided to get a Master's Degree in it.

Before starting on my Master's, I took a year off to breathe and focus on my career. I began working at Merrill Lynch at 19 years old, and although it was hard working full time while also attending school full time, it gave me a leg up in the job market when I completed my undergrad degree. Upon graduation, I was offered a position as a creative writer and marketing services manager at an insurance company and was put on the fast track to leadership.

I loved the work I was doing, and the company fulfilled its promise to cross-train me and provide new opportunities for growth on a regular basis. They also supported me in pursuing my graduate degree while working full-time. In my time working there, I went from marketing and creative writing to project management, back to marketing in a leadership role, and then into sales leadership. The final position I held with that organization involved a relocation from my home state of Florida to the Northeast, and I settled in Stamford, Connecticut, just outside New York City. It was a tough adjustment, but I eventually acclimated and kept climbing the ladder to career success!

I learned a lot in my nearly seven years at that company and took the knowledge and skills I attained with me when I was eventually recruited to a new company. And then another. And then another. As I continued to climb, my paychecks got larger, and my titles got bigger, but I started to become sick and unhappy. I didn't understand why. I had everything I had worked hard for—a great career in sales and marketing leadership, making more money than I ever thought I would. But something was missing, I just couldn't put my finger on it. Why should I be miserable when I was "successful" and had financial freedom?

That's when the zig-zagging and journey to true self-discovery began. I say "began" loosely because I clearly zig-zagged in college when determining my major, but this was another major pivot. Dealing with a plethora of health issues, I went back to school and got certified as a holistic health coach, where I learned how food, the environment, and our mindset all affect our health and well-being. I also discovered that many of my health problems were related to an undiagnosed food allergy and stress. So. I began eating differently and changing my self-care practices, and—wouldn't you know—I started getting better. Not only was I healthier, but I was also dropping weight without trying.

There were still some health issues that kept cropping up, even though the doctors said there was nothing wrong with me. Turns out, my health problems had nothing to do with diet or exercise at all; they were related to my work, more specifically, to my lack of purpose in what I was doing. Sure, I liked marketing just fine. I loved the hospital where I worked and the people I worked with. It wasn't like I wasn't doing meaningful work; it's just that I wasn't fulfilling my purpose. But it would take me several more years of trial and error to realize exactly what that purpose is.

Before I get to my purpose, I'd like to *rewind* a bit and share a few key anecdotes to give you more context.

When I was in high school, I started to notice a pattern. People who needed to talk, get things off their chest, or were seeking advice or help would come to me—both friends and acquaintances. I eventually gained the moniker "Shrink Shannon," and people told me I should become a therapist for a living. I loved helping others with problems big and small and have always felt tremendous joy when doing so, so I wore the nickname as a badge of honor. This pattern of attracting others who need help has continued into adulthood, and I am happy to support others whenever and however I can.

In high school and college, I volunteered to teach vacation bible school. My favorite part of that experience was building bonds with the kids I was helping to learn, grow, and satiate their curiosity. Watching the "light bulbs" click on when a student finally "got" something was incredibly fulfilling—something I experienced when teaching college students as well.

The same held true when I was teaching dance. I loved watching my dancers grow and evolve. It was satisfying to see them improve their skills and boost their confidence. The excitement they exuded when they finally nailed that double turn or flawlessly executed the routine was incredibly fulfilling for me. It's not like I was the one performing—they were—but their success was my success, and it brought me loads of joy.

Finally, in grad school, one of my professors told me that I was a phenomenal speaker and should pursue public speaking as a profession. I asked, *"That's a job?"* and he said yes. It felt too intangible for me—it's not like companies post full-time jobs for public speakers—so I pushed it aside and kept climbing the proverbial ladder in a more traditional sense. One with safety, security, and a regular paycheck that paid the bills.

Fast forward back to my time working at the hospital.

After completing my health coaching certification and getting my own health on track, I felt the pull to use that newfound knowledge to help others. I knew how impactful self-care, nutrition, and the mind-body connection were to overall well-being, and I wanted to share that with others. So, I quit my job, wrote a book on self-care, and became a health coach. My parents thought I was out of my mind for leaving my six-figure career, my husband was supportive but cautious, and my friends and colleagues were shocked.

In addition to beginning a health coaching business, I also chased a dream I had always wanted to accomplish—teaching. After a rigorous search and application process, I landed a job teaching communication courses at the college level. I started by teaching several undergrad courses at Iona College and then went on to teach a graduate-level course at Columbia University. I loved watching my students learn new things, expand their knowledge, and grow as people. It is an incredibly rewarding experience to know that you're opening minds and hearts and playing an important role in someone's development.

You'd think by this point in my long journey, I would have realized that being a coach is what I was meant to do. This pattern of deriving joy and fulfillment from helping others had been prominent throughout my entire life—from the time I was a kid to my corporate life, to mentoring and volunteering, to the classroom and health coaching. I think I knew at this point in time that I was called to inspire and coach others, but I still hadn't landed on the right type of coaching, so I wasn't there quite yet.

You see, it turned out health coaching wasn't really for me. I knew I enjoyed the coaching aspect, and I love health and wellness, I just didn't love health coaching as a career. But a funny thing happened as I was in the throes of yet another "what do I want to be when I grow up" moment—my career found me.

It happened gradually and without me even realizing it at first. I was working in a co-working space surrounded by entrepreneurs and business owners who had to do presentations on a regular basis. The community there knew I taught public speaking and communication classes at the college level, so I regularly received requests from fellow entrepreneurs to help them with their pitches, decks, sales interactions, and more. I found these sidebars a welcome break from health coaching and, me being me, helped out free of charge.

I started looking forward to helping out in this capacity more than doing health coaching, and that's when I realized that my energy was aligned with communication coaching. That's when I finally listened and answered the call. That's when I stepped into my purpose and used my God-given talents to help people unearth the potential that was deep within them and share their message with the world. That's when Shannon Malkin Daniels, Public Speaking, Communication and Confidence Coach, was born. And that's when I began living my optimal life.

You see, for me, living an optimal life means fulfilling your purpose. It's doing work that's meaningful and helping others. We all have our own unique talents, and each of us has a different purpose to fulfill. Living an optimal life is fulfilling that purpose, even if it means bucking the status quo, taking a risk, and stepping outside of your comfort zone.

Society tells us we should be one thing, but many of us feel trapped or stagnated when we follow that path. I know I did. It wasn't until I stopped resisting the call and started living my purpose that I began to live my optimal life. Not answering the call—or worse, living life for others—kept me from living my optimal life for too long.

So I challenge you to dig deep and ask yourself: Are you fulfilling your purpose? If not, you're not living your optimal life. I know that may be shocking to read, but it's true. How can you live your optimal life if you're not doing what you were designed to do? Once I came to that realization, stepped out on faith, and answered the call to fulfill my purpose, I stepped into my power.

As a public speaking, communication and confidence coach, I now get to help people every single day while doing something I love. I am blessed with a gift to see things within people that they may not see in themselves, then help them to not only see it as well, but believe it and own it. When my clients thank me for helping them overcome their fear and anxiety around speaking, nail a keynote speech, become a TEDx phenomenon, get booked on Shark Tank, land a big account, or boost their confidence, I tell them that I didn't do it, *they* did. The confidence and capability to do all of those things lived in them all along; I just helped to pull it out and nurture it.

To boil it down, I coach and assist others in their pursuit of an optimal life, which in turn allows me to live my own optimal life.

Integration

If you're not living your optimal life, I challenge you to ask yourself WHY. Grab a pen and paper, and answer the following questions:

- What is my **purpose** in life?
- Am I fulfilling my purpose? If not, why?
- What is holding me back from living my optimal life? Fear? Insecurity? Something else?
- What is one change I can make **today** to fulfill my purpose and live my optimal life?

If you need help figuring out the answers to these questions, turn to a friend or mentor, or hire a coach to help you. I've had many coaches and mentors over the years, and I wouldn't be where I am today without them—I wouldn't have figured out my purpose. And I wouldn't be living my optimal life.

About Shannon

"It wasn't until I stopped resisting the call and started living my purpose that I began to live my optimal life."

Shannon Malkin Daniels is a communication nerd, entrepreneur, best-selling author, and captivating TEDx speaker. Embracing challenges as opportunities, she proves that with a potent blend of creativity, hard work, and perseverance, anything is achievable. Her self-published book, "Water Yourself," has transcended borders, touching readers in 10 countries, and is now evolving into an eagerly awaited 3-day wellness retreat.

Armed with a master's degree in interpersonal communication from the esteemed University of Central Florida, Shannon's academic prowess intertwines seamlessly with her hands-on experience. She has graced the faculties of prestigious institutions like Columbia University and Iona College, while also excelling as a mentor for executives, entrepreneurs, and students, helping them master the art of effective communication and public speaking.

In 2018, Shannon's visionary spirit led her to establish encaptiv, an award-winning platform revolutionizing audience engagement and conversion for virtual, hybrid, and in-person presentations and events. Her ventures continue to shape the landscape of communication, leaving a trail of inspiration and success.

Connect with Shannon:

SPEAC Success
Public Speaking, Communication
& Confidence Coaching
www.speacsuccess.com
Email: speac@speacsuccess.com
Phone: 844.489.2837

Chapter 14

Reclaiming My Identity

Shontelle Brewster

It was a hot summer day in Barbados. The annoying screeching sound of the old fan blowing the leaves from my homework book was drowned out by playful screams from the neighborhood kids playing and the faint sound of a dog barking in the distance. My brother, a young, tall, bootleg version of my father, was on his way out to pick fruits with his friends.

Suddenly, the sound of a child crying snapped me out of my daze. It was one of my little sisters. She was tired and hungry. In that frozen moment in time, I vividly remember asking myself why me? Why can't I play with my friends like a normal person? Why am I cleaning poop and wiping snot? How come, my brother, who is older, didn't have the responsibilities I do? I guess I was supposed to feel lucky that nobody ever asked me if I had homework or had to ask permission to eat what I wanted.

I often daydreamed about my father and wondered if he was alive and if I would have all these responsibilities. I was angry at him for leaving me. I was angry at my mother for going to work—I was angry at everyone. Still, I wanted to be a good daughter and hoped that one day I would be rewarded if not recognized for being a good girl, but it never happened.

You will never amount to nothing and *You're going to get pregnant early* were my broken records. That was the only attention I got from other relatives. The exception was my favorite auntie;

she told me that she believed I could be a teacher, although she would prefer it if I were a flight attendant. Unfortunately, it wasn't long before my grades started to reflect how I was feeling inside. I disliked school, and although it was a brief escape, my never-ending responsibilities were always waiting for me like a secret friend.

My name is Shontelle Brewster, and I was a *parentified* child.

What does it mean to be both a caregiver and child, responsible for nurturing others while shouldering the weight of poverty?

The term parentified may appear to be a challenging concept at first glance. Still, for myself and countless others across the globe, it is a deeply traumatic experience that carries multiple profound consequences for an individual's sense of self and their understanding of relationships.

My journey to discovering my true self started with my migration to the United States. My siblings were now at the age where they could fend for themselves, and I was left to pick up the pieces of my life and start the healing process. The truth is, I had no idea how to accomplish that. The only thing I knew was that I needed to get away from my family home at the first opportunity. I also thought that maybe if I just moved on and forgot about it, my issues would just resolve themselves.

A couple of years later, I got pregnant with my first child and moved to another state. Years afterward, I got married, still at a very young age, and then I got pregnant with my daughter. It was fun in the beginning. After all, I was an experienced caregiver. It didn't take long for me to realize that I was recycled into the same situation I grew up in. Taking care of my children was a no-brainer, but having to take care of his father as if he were a child was not what I signed up for. I had difficulty setting boundaries, prioritizing my own needs, and displaying co-dependent tendencies.

Once again, I found myself asking, "Why me?" Here I was as an adult, still seeking validation and perhaps would be willing to trade my peace for some acknowledgment of my efforts. I wanted to be a good wife.

Someone once said, "Your trauma is not your fault, but your healing is your responsibility." I was with a partner who was verbally and mentally abusive. I cringed at the thought of telling my friends and family what I was going through. After all, it looks like I may beat the odds. I was worried about what they would think, *She can't even keep her marriage.*

The shadow of imposter syndrome was looming like a dark cloud on a rainy day. I thought, perhaps, that prayer would work. So, I prayed and prayed some more. Those prayers went unanswered—or so I thought. Instead, I was given a gift. That gift came in the form of the ability to look within myself. It didn't take long for me to start to realize that I was in control of how my story would be written. I left and never looked back.

This was the first tangible start to my healing journey. Still, I felt lost, empty inside, and unsure of who I was or who I was supposed to be. All I knew was that I did not feel good inside. The researcher in me went online, and I started reading about how to take care of your mental health. I read self-help books which were online in the form of articles, and as I listened to and read people's stories, I read something that would change my life forever.

In bold Times New Roman font, there was a statement that read, "Using self-help tools and books could be helpful, but it is important to seek professional advice to deeper explore your symptoms." The answer was staring me right in the face. Therapy. But wait—I thought. What would people think? This is taboo in my culture. I was afraid of being judged or labeled as weak or, worse, insane. I was afraid of opening up to a stranger—how could they possibly understand? As I pondered on this critical decision, I wondered again, if I let enough time pass, maybe I would get better.

I am happy to say that putting myself in therapy was the best decision I have ever made in my life. At that time, this was my dark secret. Although this therapist did not look like me nor understand my culture, it still was a good stepping stone for me to dive into my healing journey. This is what helped me see myself as this powerful being who is more than a caregiver or told I wouldn't be anything in life. This was my rebirth.

It is interesting how God has a funny way of sending you messages. While working as a Medical Assistant at a local hospital in Connecticut, I did not feel fulfilled. The best part of my shift was talking to the patients, who I believe saw me as an outlet or as someone other than an MA who took care of their endocrine issues. Patients would share information about family drama and emotional and mental issues they were experiencing, and I would listen and sometimes offer suggestions. One day, a patient looked at me and said, "Girl, you are in the wrong field. You should be a therapist." I smiled and said thank you.

That day, I went home and started my research on how to become a therapist. Going through the different paths of the profession, Marriage and Family Therapy caught my attention because it focused more on relational issues and systemic frameworks, which resonated with me. I looked up the requirements to become a Marriage and Family Therapist (MFT) and then started my journey into becoming one.

As I reminisced on the day of graduation, all I felt was gratitude. I reflected on the days and nights I spent studying. I had a son and daughter to take care of while maintaining a home as a single mother with a full-time job. It was a big deal for me to receive my Master's Degree because it solidified what I knew to be true about me. I am intelligent.

Why was this important to me? Well, let's start with being told all the things I was told as a child. So yeah, in a way, it felt good showing those individuals that they didn't break me. I beat the odds. It was an amazing feeling knowing that I was the first grandchild to receive a master's, and, in my family, this was a huge accomplishment.

Was my journey over? Did I finally accomplish all that I wanted to accomplish? Was my trauma resolved? Absolutely not! Breaking generational patterns was now a conscious effort. Imagine, as a young woman, having to unlearn, relearn, learn, and let go of unhealthy patterns that plagued my entire being. Things that I grew up seeing family members do just did not sit well with me, and though I was a young teen trying to be someone other than unkind, there were times this took over.

Being a product of your environment can either be a good thing or a bad thing. In my case, it was both. As a child, I was always yelled at and was never heard. I found myself yelling at others to be heard. I had to unlearn being overly critical. I no longer focus on perfectionism. Self-critical habits and the constant fear of failure are not allowed in my home. I had to unlearn negativity and complaining and instead adopt an optimistic point of view on life. I had to unlearn bad habits that led to a lack of financial responsibility while balancing privileged behavior in my children. Finally, I had to learn that it is okay to express yourself in healthier, kinder ways.

I discovered that you could spare the rod without spoiling the child. Today, we no longer have the excuse our parents had, *"We didn't know better."* My children have a safe space in me. They can share their thoughts and feelings about most things, and I pride myself on this because I never had that! I do not spank my children; I do not ignore my children, and my children are not forced to make adult decisions. My son is not forced to take care of his sister as his responsibility. Instead, he takes care of his little sister in the capacity he can at his current age and developmental stage. I make sure I am aware of how my children are doing in school with their academics and behavior. I make sure I check in on homework and that they are doing assignments and handing them in on time. I help them with a vast number of different things, which helps us stay bonded.

Being parentified taught me grace. I learned to have grace for my mother, especially because, in retrospect, she truly did the best she could. Though I did not agree with the way she treated me at times, I can now understand that she, too, was dealing with a lot. It taught me how to be a responsible adult. I matured fast and was given a gift of emotional intelligence, empathy, and understanding. I learned self-sufficiency and always had natural problem-solving abilities, and by addressing my issues, I now have stronger family bonds. I learned that my trials and tribulations do not define who I truly am as a person, and I honor my trauma for that reason.

My name is Shontelle Brewster, and I am a parentified child who is healed.

I am intelligent, I am gifted, and I can do difficult things. I am a woman with unwavering strength and perseverance. I am a resilient woman who has faced so many adversities, and though I wanted to give up, I kept going. I am a mother, a daughter, a sister, a cousin, a friend, a therapist, a college professor, an award-winner, and an amazing person. I am becoming who the higher power wants me to be.

Integration

- Take some time to write about your experiences as a parentified child. What were the responsibilities and roles you took on in your family? How did this impact your childhood and development? Consider the emotions, challenges, and strengths that emerged from this role. Reflecting on these experiences can help you gain clarity and insight into your journey.

- Write about the person you would like to be outside of the parentified role. Imagine a life where you have the freedom to pursue your own dreams, needs, and desires. What does this version of yourself look like? How would you like to redefine your identity? Explore your passions, interests, and goals that may have been put on hold while taking care of others. Emphasize self-care, self-discovery, and personal growth as you envision a future where you can prioritize your own well-being.

- Consider the boundaries you would like to establish in your relationships, both with your family and others. Reflect on how being parentified has influenced your understanding of boundaries and how it has affected your ability to say no or prioritize your own needs. Write about specific instances where you would like to set boundaries and explore strategies for doing so assertively and respectfully. This prompt can help you redefine your relationship dynamics and cultivate healthier interactions with others.

About Shontelle

"I was given a gift. That gift came in the form of the ability to look within myself. It didn't take long for me to start to realize that I was in control of how my story would be written."

Shontelle Brewster is the CEO of Love & Light Wellness Therapy located in Connecticut. She holds a Master's degree in Marriage and Family Therapy from Central Connecticut State University. Shontelle is a co-host on a local radio station, using the platform to discuss many mental health topics, including self-care. She is also an Adjunct Professor at the University of Hartford where she teaches Sociology of Health and Illness. Ms. Brewster's passion for supporting trauma survivors stems from a deep desire to empower individuals and provide a safe space for healing. She has witnessed firsthand the transformative power of therapy in helping individuals process their trauma, build resilience, and reclaim their lives.

Additionally, as a therapist with a focus on Caribbean first and second-generation immigrants, she recognizes the complex intersection of cultural identity, family dynamics, and acculturation struggles.

Connect with Shontelle:
Love & Light Wellness Therapy
www.tellshontelle.com
Email: sbrewster@llwt.info

CHAPTER 15

"MARTHA, GET OUT OF THE KITCHEN"

ROBIN H. CLARE

Service

One morning at sunrise on the beach, The Divine asked me a simple question,

"Robin, do you think that spiritual seekers have lived their extraordinary lives for their own entertainment?"

I laughed and said, "Well, we have some seriously entertaining stories to tell."

The Divine replied, "That may be true, but we need our spiritual seekers to stop seeking and start serving."

Throughout your adult life, you will have the opportunity to serve others in many different ways. You can serve your family, boss, clients, higher power, and yourself. But what does it mean to be of true service? To be of true service is to support the welfare of another person or group in an unconditional manner.

The following excerpt from *The Christ Blueprint* by Padma Aon Prakasha defines true service:

"Service is never a burden; it is a lightness. Service is never a duty—it is a voluntary willingness. Service includes all of you and does not leave anything else. Service is not something you do; it is a way of life. It is the Divine's lifestyle. It is our nature, our birthright, and our completion

into love. If you think you are in service and you are not enjoying it, then it is not your true service."

Even as a little girl, my uncle had a nickname for me; he would call me "Fetch-it." If he needed a tool from the barn, I would run off to find it and bring it to him. I learned that as a female, I was here to serve others, and as I grew into a young woman, I was often confused about service to men. There was often a blurring of the lines between service and my integrity.

As a woman in corporate America in the 1980s, we desperately tried to break the glass ceiling. This required a combination of ruthlessness, smarts, sexiness, and a service mindset with your eye on your next accomplishment and reward. Service in this way was very self-centered and not selfless like true service.

During this time, I also stepped onto my spiritual path. And for many years, I felt utterly inauthentic. I was a spiritual warrior on the weekends and a corporate warrior during the week. I had no idea how to bring my spirituality to my corporate life, so I left my well-compensated corporate job to start a career in the spiritual arts.

I was a spiritual business promoter for many years, ensuring that other spiritual teachers were successful. Then, one day, I received a message from Yeshua (Jesus) to write a book with him entitled *Messiah Within—A Guide to Embracing Your Inner Divinity.* This was not an easy task because I was not an author, religious scholar, or spiritual expert. But beyond the apparent impediments above, there was an even bigger one: I was over-committed to my family life, and I would prioritize them over writing the book.

When I ignored my commitment to write the book due to my family obligations, Yeshua would come to me and say, *"Martha, get out of the kitchen."* At first, I wondered who Martha was and why Yeshua would identify me as her. Here is an excerpt from the New Testament:

"Now as they were traveling along, He entered a village; and a woman named Martha welcomed Him into her home. She had a sister called Mary, who was seated at the Lord's feet, listening to His word. But Martha was distracted with all her preparations; and she came up to Him and said, 'Lord, do You not care that my sister has left me to do all the serving alone? Then tell her to help me.' But the Lord answered and said to her, 'Martha, Martha, you are worried and bothered about so many things; but only one thing is necessary, for Mary has chosen the good part, which shall not be taken away from her." (Luke 10:38-42, NASB)

At that moment, Yeshua asked Martha to prioritize the spiritual path over ensuring the perfect meal. How often do we think the mundane day-to-day tasks are of greater value than our relationship with our inner divinity? And yet it is essential to give Martha props for having the courage to ask Yeshua for what she needed.

As I studied Martha, an important woman in Yeshua's story, I discovered that she identified with the concept of service. In my journey during my corporate days, service was provided as a means to get a more prestigious job and more money. In my spiritual promoter days, I tried to make a living by serving the community. This did not work out well for me.

I discovered that the *harder* I tried to make money in the spiritual arts, the *less* money I made. The Divine gave me a very clear message. "Success is measured by Impact, and Impact is rewarded with Abundance." Until I could take this concept to heart and determine my value proposition, I would not achieve financial success, especially in the spiritual arts.

Impact in the Spiritual Arts is not about how many tickets you sell to an event; it is about how the content and wisdom that you are sharing change the lives of others. Therefore, in the spiritual arts (and almost any business endeavor), the more significantly you impact your clients and customers, the more you will be rewarded with abundance.

Next, the question becomes, what does abundance mean to you? Is it enough money and time to do what you love? Or will you get caught in the endless loop of service and money rewards like one experiences in corporate America? Finding the balance of true service to clients, customers, family, community, and yourself will ultimately lead you to a joyous life and the freedom many of us crave.

I have received lists of words from the Divine throughout my spiritual journey. The following list is one that I gave the title, *The Six Stages of Spiritual Success*. I am including this list in this chapter because it applies to spiritual seekers looking to find out how they can best serve. If you changed the words to fit your situation, you would see that these six stages apply to any form of success.

1. **AWARENESS**: The first stage begins when you realize there is more to this life than you can experience through your five senses. This sixth sense connects you to a knowing that there is a presence available to you beyond the confines of your daily life. This warm, loving presence called Spirit or the Divine has always been a part of your life; you just may not have been aware.

2. **COMMITMENT**: The second stage begins when you just must know more about this extraordinary presence in your life. You begin to read, take classes, and converse with others. Regardless of the reaction of others, you tenaciously stay on your path. In this stage, synchronistic events become more prevalent in your life as the Divine begins to communicate with you.

3. **MASTERY:** The third stage begins when you move from a solid curiosity to a total commitment to becoming the spiritual person you keep reading about in books or listening to in class. You dive deeper into the teachings of Spiritual Masters, and you begin to heal the traumas from this lifetime and past lifetimes. Spiritual Seekers love to seek and often get stuck in the mastery stage. Moving beyond mastery is vital because you are required to serve as well!

4. SERVICE: If you are on your spiritual journey, you are on this planet to serve. Fortunately, you have opportunities to help yourself, your family, your community, and our world. You can serve in both your personal and professional life. For example, you can serve others by simply holding the door open for another or by creating a service business. Just know the more you act, the more you emulate the Divine.

5. LEADERSHIP: By this stage of your spiritual journey, you have gathered a deep understanding of spiritual concepts, a service mindset, and a desire to integrate spirituality into your moment-to-moment living. When you become out of alignment with the Divine, you re-align in a faster, more graceful time frame. By living a dedicated spiritual life, you naturally lead others along their spiritual journey.

6. FREEDOM: In this last stage, you are rewarded for all your dedication to your spiritual journey with love, peace, joy, and abundance. Divine *love* is experienced by a whole heart that unconditionally shares love. Divine *peace* is practiced by knowing you are never alone and are One with the Divine. Divine *joy* is accomplished by seeing the world through the Divine's positive lens. Divine *abundance* is achieved by impacting others' lives through unwavering service.

After connecting to the energy of Martha (or true service) while writing my first book, I often wondered when I would connect to Martha more significantly in my life or another way of saying it when I would live a life of day-to-day service. I never realized that this could be accomplished outside the boundaries of my spiritual business.

Throughout my career as a spiritual messenger, I told client after client that committing your life to serving the Divine did not require you to work in the spiritual arts. I must have said this to every client, yet I never thought that was possible for me. If I went back into the "real world" to work, I would relinquish my spiritual identity and connection to the Divine.

This year, I decided to venture into the "real world" and apply for a position I knew would be a perfect fit. I accepted the part-time position as the Executive Director of the Seniors Job Bank serving Greater Hartford. The mission of the Seniors Job Bank is to connect individuals over 50 years of age with opportunities for part-time work either in business, with homeowners, or in municipalities.

In this role, I feel of great service and that I am doing good deeds all day. This "normal" job is probably the most spiritual role I have ever had. This astounded me because I was constantly serving the Divine and the community over the past twenty years in the spiritual arts. However, I have realized that I am truly embracing the energy of Martha or the significance of service at the Seniors Job Bank.

Why does the work at the Seniors Job Bank feel more like the energy of Martha? I believe this because I have stepped out into the public arena, serving people I might never have known and having more compassion and patience than I thought possible. I have discovered that "Spiritual Robin" can show up at the Seniors Job Bank.

That means that I have embodied the spiritual teachings and the life of service as demonstrated by Martha. Every day, I chuckle at the unfolding of synchronicities in the office. For example, a business requires a particular skill set for a position our current service providers don't have. I send the request out to Universe, and within a short time, a new service provider with the skill set shows up.

The synchronicities work in the opposite manner as well; a new or existing service provider will ask me if we have an opening for their unique skill set; unfortunately, we don't. I send this request out to the Universe, and within a short time, a request comes in from a job owner for that skill set.

The funny part is that these synchronistic events surprise me every time, yet I know that this is part of the *Six Spiritual Stages of Success*. In the sixth stage of Freedom, Divine *abundance* is achieved by impacting others' lives through unwavering service. This service mindset is happening simultaneously by the service provider, the job owner, and the Seniors Job Bank. As a result, everyday miracles become the business standard.

In the Old Testament, the literal meaning of the word Mitzvah is commandment. The more accepted definition of a Mitzvah is a good deed. One can have thoughts of good deeds, but a Mitzvah is to be of true service with genuine compassion and a heartfelt desire to help. To me, being of true joyful service and making an impact on the lives of others while still being a loving "Martha in my kitchen" with my family is what living the *ultimate life* is all about.

Integration

- Looking at the six stages of spiritual success (awareness, commitment, mastery, service, leadership, and freedom), which stage do you feel most connected with now?
- What is one action you can take to go deeper into your current stage of spiritual success?
- Are you eager to step into a new stage of spiritual success? If so, what is one action you can take to move into that next stage?

About Robin

"In the spiritual arts (and almost any business endeavor), the more significantly you impact your clients and customers, the more you will be rewarded with abundance."

Robin H. Clare's path to fulfilling her destiny began by leaving her traditional 25-year MBA business career and traveling the globe to study with spiritual masters. But first, Robin had to reveal her deep secret of struggling for four decades with food addiction and bulimia. Now in grounded recovery, Robin is an award-winning coach, recovery medium, best-selling spiritual author, and highly regarded speaker and teacher. In addition, she is the Executive Director for the Seniors Job Bank of Greater Hartford.

She has documented her extraordinary spiritual journey in the highly-acclaimed, followed by Amazon bestsellers, and in 2021, she released an ebook and recorded divine meditations in. She will release *The Hidden Truth Within Trauma* in 2023. Awards include 10 Best Life/Business Coaches and 10 Best Energy Healers in the Natural Nutmeg Readers Polls of 2017-2022. Certifications include Recovery Coach Professional™, Advanced Akashic Record reader, Reiki Master, 13th Octave LaHoChi practitioner, and National Speakers Academy certified keynote speaker. Robin is a channel for the Ascended Masters.

Connect with Robin:

www.clare-ity.squarespace.com
IG: @clareitybyrobin
FB: @clareitywithrobin

PART V

GROWTH

Chapter 16

I Am in Control of My Money Story

LaQueshia Clemons

I could not wait to get a credit card when I turned 18. I applied for my first credit card the day after my birthday and was approved for three thousand dollars. I thought this was great, I could get name-brand clothes, shoes, purses, and more now that I have a credit card. My mother always told me that I could get the things I wanted and pay if off over time. She made sure to tell me never to be late and at least pay the minimum balance on my credit cards.

When I would go to the mall and be offered a store credit card because I would get 20 percent off, I would sign up for the credit card. I racked up credit card debt fairly quickly by the age of 25. I had over 25 thousand dollars of credit card debt and could not keep up with the payments. I was working full-time but was never able to save money. My emotions were all over the place because I felt depressed and anxious about money. I was worried about how I was going to pay for my day-to-day living. I couldn't enjoy social outings with friends because I was putting everything on a credit card and not able to afford anything.

I got to a point where I couldn't make on-time payments to one credit card and missed three months of payments. I looked at other family members, such as my aunts and cousins and they talked about repossession of cars, bad credit scores, and also not being able to make their bill payments I thought this was normal, and if I didn't pay it, then it would eventually go away.

Well, I quickly learned that was not true. The creditors were calling me a lot because they wanted to collect payment or make an arrangement with me. I was desperate and looked into a debt management company but I did not follow through on them because I wasn't willing to not make payments on the creditors I was on time with. I finally picked up the phone and talked to my credit card company and found out that they have programs within their company to work on bringing my payments current.

At this point, I couldn't understand why I had no extra money to do anything with. I felt miserable and awful. I started questioning myself as to why this was happening. I thought I needed to make more money so I could get out of this, but that wasn't what I needed to do. I needed to understand why this was happening. After reading books and watching YouTube videos, I reflected upon my life as to where it was before and where it was going. I soon realized that my money decisions were because of what I grew up around. I reflected upon my close family and their relationship with money. I started to be okay with not paying my credit card bills on time because I was overwhelmed and wanted to avoid them.

At one point, I had prided myself on being able to take care of stuff, so I couldn't believe I had let my finances get this bad. When my credit score started to fall because I wasn't paying my credit card bills, they were trying to collect money from me. I couldn't just let this go. I couldn't understand how people within my family were okay with the creditors always calling and their credit scores falling significantly. But the reality is my family avoided it and was okay with not having good credit and missing a bill or two. I realized that this had become our culture, and we accepted living this way and thought it was normal.

After reading many books and doing a lot of research, I learned that I had to figure out what my values were and set financial goals. I realized that I was spending money just to spend it. I didn't value my money. I didn't buy things that made me feel good and meant a lot to me. I was buying items just because I could. Once I was able to finalize what my values were and started setting goals for my money, things started to change. I put boundaries in place with family and friends around money. I started telling my family that our money choices were unhealthy and we needed to shift our money mindset.

I was on a financially free journey and had to be okay with setting boundaries to hit my goals. I was determined to get on the right financial path for myself and my immediate family. I wanted to live a life where I could travel without putting everything on a credit card and having to pay it off over time. I was able to accomplish my goals, pay off debt, and learn financial literacy. I was able to learn how to invest and build my credit. I learned where I valued putting my money. I was able to get out of credit card debt, and today I can say I am living the financially free journey I desired to live.

As a therapist in 2017, I was meeting with clients who had some financial difficulties. I started noticing that, culturally they were dealing with the same things that I was dealing with. Lots of debt, no financial guidance, or taking money from the electric bill to pay the rent and then taking money from the cable bill to pay the electric. These were unhealthy money cycles that clients were stuck in. I was speaking with clients who had no desire to get off of state assistance or make more money because, for them, this was normal and the right thing to do from what they grew up around. Some clients did not know anyone who did not receive any assistance from the state, so they were afraid to not have the security net of public assistance.

I wanted to bring money and therapy together but wasn't sure how. I went on a Google search and found the Financial Therapy

Association. They defined it as "a process informed by both therapeutic and financial competencies that helps people think, feel, communicate, and behave differently with money to improve overall well-being through evidence-based practices and interventions." I then started discovering terms such as "financial trauma" and "money stories." I realized that I had gone through all of this and now could help my clients through it.

I overcame my financial trauma by paying off my credit card debt and being responsible for using my credit card debt. I now use credit cards every day to benefit me. I pay my card off every month in full and take full advantage of all the credit card perks. I am now able to travel for free using points. I have had flights to Aruba and other places for free. I have stayed in hotels for free and received free upgrades at these hotels. I took the time to learn how credit cards work and also learn how credit card companies make money. The credit card companies want you to pay interest on their cards and attempt to entice you by offering points towards free things such as travel. It is great that they have so many good benefits, however, if you pay interest on anything you put on a credit card, then your points are useless.

As a result, of the experience I went through, I have been able to help many clients overcome their financial trauma and understand their money stories.

For example, I worked with Jill for one year to help her overcome her financial anxieties. Jill had worked very hard most of her adult life and finally got a job where she was making six figures. Before getting this job, she struggled to make ends meet and sometimes struggled to buy food. As a result of this, Jill developed a scarcity mindset towards money. She was afraid to spend money out of fear of going back to a time when she didn't have much money.

While working with this client, I was able to help her understand her money story and to make her feel more secure and confident in her money decisions. Her biggest goal was to return to Europe, where she studied abroad to visit her close friends that she hadn't been able to visit with for several years due to her money struggles. After six months of working with me, Jill was able to go to Europe and feel secure about her money and also spent money in Europe. She was tearful but happy that she was able to hit her money goals.

Despite all the money challenges, we can all live our optimal lives. Our money story may get created and formed as a child, but you have the ability to rewrite your money story to what you want.

Integration

- Digging deep and reflecting upon what means the most to you, ask yourself, what are your values?
- What is my money story?
- How can I rewrite my money story?

About LaQueshia

"Despite all the money challenges, we can all live our optimal lives. You have the ability to rewrite your money story to what you want."

LaQueshia Clemons is a Licensed Clinical Social Worker (LCSW) and an Accredited Financial Counselor(AFC). She earned her Master's Degree from Springfield College in Massachusetts. She works as a Financial Therapist within her own private practice (www.freedomlifetherapy.com), where she focuses on individuals' and couples' emotional and behavioral habits around personal finance. As a dynamic and skilled social worker, beginning in 2010, she began her career working with youth and families across the lifespan in a variety of settings. LaQueshia is currently focused on delivering workshops and speeches to individuals to help them understand their money story and the impact it has on their lives.

Connect with LaQueshia:
www.freedomlifetherapy.com
101 Centerpoint Drive
Suite 214
Middletown, CT
Email: admin@freedomlifetherapy.com
Phone: 860.578.4597

CHAPTER 17

YOUR BUSINESS ONLY NEEDS TO MAKE SENSE TO YOU

AMBER DANCY

"That makes perfect sense!" If you ever hear me talk or if you ever work with me, you'll hear me use this phrase. I use it all the time because understanding how things work is one of my superpowers. Things make sense to me until they don't. From the outside looking in, much of my story might not make sense to others. To me, though, each decision made sense until it didn't anymore.

I grew up in a small town about an hour north of Memphis, Tennessee. I loved growing up in the country. Life was simple and filled with playing outdoors, getting lost in the woods, and riding my bike to the local store down the street. By the time I got to high school, I had no idea what I wanted to be when I grew up. I was a young girl in the middle of farm country. I could join the Future Farmers of America (FFA) or Health Occupations Students of America (HOSA). I didn't play sports and had no other ideas on what type of career I really wanted. I knew I didn't want to be a farmer or work with animals, so I joined HOSA and decided to be a nurse. I became a Certified Nurse's Assistant

(CNA) instead of working in fast food jobs in my teenage years. It made perfect sense!

Fast forward to the end of high school, I met my future husband at age 17. I graduated high school, started nursing school, and got married all within the space of a year. Then something really interesting happened. My new husband decided that he might want to join the military, the Air Force to be specific. I went with him to the recruiter's office with the intention of keeping him from doing anything "crazy." To this day, I can't really tell you what that recruiter said but I was the first one signing the enlistment paperwork. I'm pretty sure whatever he said made perfect sense, at least to me!

One of the processes for getting a "job" in the military is for each person to take the Armed Services Vocational Aptitude Battery (ASVAB) test. My scores were a turning point in my life. I scored very high in mechanical aptitude. Combine that fact with timing, and that's how I became a mechanic instead of a nurse. You see, my husband and I wanted to go to basic training together, and the only jobs available were mechanical. Again, choosing this path made perfect sense. We joined the Air Force, and I spent the next six years as a female in a predominantly male career field. I learned about diesel engines, how to read electrical schematics, and even how to change oil and tires on vehicles. I learned much, much more about myself along the way.

Life kept going, as life does, and I got pregnant with our son in year five of my military enlistment. I could not do any part of my job while pregnant due to safety. My leadership did what they normally do with pregnant females and put me in an administrative position. I mean, it makes perfect sense, right?! I got to experience what it's like to be in a support position to military leaders and used my "understanding things" superpower to learn about operations.

I left the military the next year and became a commander's secretary as a civil servant. From that point, I worked many secretarial roles and then moved on to administrative and office management roles, and then to operations manager roles. Every move to the next role made perfect sense to me. Some moves were because we physically moved to a new place, or for more money, or because I was bored in the role, or for advancement of a job title. Every decision made sense until it didn't.

I left the "corporate" job scene in March of 2020, just as the world began shutting down for the pandemic. I spent several years building a business that mirrored the work I did in operations. *Makes sense, huh?!* I took my skills and built a thriving business serving other business owners with their operations needs. I helped them build their businesses and create their success. And secretly, I was dying a little inside. It felt like I had traded one job for four jobs. I was working the way that made sense. I built a business that made perfect sense—and it was killing me.

This was the point that I discovered that I needed things to make sense in a different way. Thus, my coaching business was born. I finally realized that the way I was working no longer worked for me. It no longer made sense to me to be a service provider. Despite having a six-figure year in year three of my business, I could no longer work inside other people's businesses in this way. I desired to help others in a different way. I realized that sometimes being rebellious is the most practical thing I could do in my business.

It was time to start living optimally in my business. It was time to start doing things in the ways that really worked for me. It was time for me to really discover what I wanted my business to look like. It was time to release the ways of business that didn't resonate with me. It was time to embrace that I knew what was best for me and I could design a business that serves me first, instead of a business that was created to serve my clients first.

It's super rebellious to consider that your business gets to serve you FIRST. We've been taught that to have a successful business, you have to do what the client wants first. You know that old saying that "the customer is always right." I highly disagree! The key to living optimally is to figure out what works for YOU first before you consider others. If it doesn't work for you, it won't work for anybody else because you will eventually burn yourself out and have to do something else. Or you will be completely miserable and not really able to serve your clients anyway. Why not start with you first and see what happens from there?!

Here's how I see it. Every business has a sweet spot. In order to find the sweet spot, we have to look at the humans in the business. There are three groups of humans in your business: you, your team, and your clients. These humans are the keys to how you make decisions about what needs to happen in your business. Each group has their own needs, desires, and expectations. In order to create successful operations and systems, we need to find the place where these three groups crossover. This allows for happy, healthy humans that want to be a part of your business. This is your Business Sweet Spot.

Many businesses start by looking at the needs, desires, and expectations of the potential customer/client first. Particularly for small businesses, this creates an imbalance between the three groups. This method is more likely to create a business that is only focused on the client, and you, the owner, get lost in the mix. What if, instead, we start by looking at what YOU need, desire, and expect first?

Your business gets to serve you first, before anyone else. You get to decide how you desire to work and how you want to do things in your business. Once you know that, hiring team members (when the time is right) and calling in clients is so much easier. You are able to clearly tell the other two groups of humans what you need, desire, and expect. They are able to clearly decide for themselves if those things will work for them. You get to work from the optimal place in your business, which will allow you to do this for the rest of your life as well.

The real secret to all of this is that you are NOT your business. You and your business are two separate entities. I'm not talking about being the "face" of your business in your marketing and messaging. I'm talking about the belief that you ARE your business. It might feel like that in the beginning. It may be really hard to look at the business outside of your personal self and capacity, but it is separate. You and your business are integrated. You are in relationship with each other. You work together towards a similar outcome. And yet, you are still two different entities. Separating myself from "being my business" allowed me to both separate my self-worth from the business success and allowed me to create a business that serves me first.

If you are reading this and feeling like you've created your business to serve others before it serves you, I see you. I hear you. Heck, I was you! The good news is that you can change this. Starting right now, you can adjust how you make decisions in your business. You can begin to shift your perspective.

1. Get out a sheet of paper.

2. Write "ME" at the top.

3. Draw a line down the middle.

4. In the left column, write down everything in your business that feels like it's working well for you. Make sure you are doing this from your perspective. The perspective of the business serving YOU first.

5. In the right column, write down all the things that feel like they aren't working. Again, do this from your perspective.

6. Take the things in the left column and do more of these. Take the things in the right column and start playing with how you want to shift them to serve YOU first.

You do not have to change everything overnight. You do not need to burn your business down and start over. Simply start shifting the ways you operate in your business to allow the business to serve you first. If it feels good, keep doing it. If it doesn't feel good, get curious about how you can shift it to feel good for you.

Integration

- What areas/processes in my business were designed with my clients first? Do these areas/processes work for me? If not, how can I begin shifting them to serve me first?
- If you have a team, have them do this exercise as well and then compare. Any areas that don't align are places to start thinking about shifting to serve both you and your team.
- What are the needs, desires, and expectations I have from my business? Is my business serving those needs, desires, and expectations? Where do I need to start looking at shifting so that my business serves me first?
- What feels really sticky in my business right now? What's not really working? Am I being really honest with myself about what I need from my business?

About Amber

"Your business gets to serve you first before anyone else. You get to decide how you desire to work and how you want to do things in your business."

Amber Dancy is an intuitive business coach and founder of Practical Rebel. She believes that sometimes rebelling is the most practical thing you can do for your life and your business. Her mission is to transform the old boring "business standards" into "human-first approaches," which allows us to create safer team relationships and allow people to show up as their whole, unique selves inside our businesses.

She proudly holds a master's degree in organizational psychology and certifications in both trauma-informed practices and Sourced leadership. She is also certified in many levels of business operations and has other psychology degrees. Amber is super skilled in the practical and people sides of business, making a natural bridge to help translate between people and process.

Connect with Amber:
Practical Rebel
www.practicalrebel.com
Email: amber@practicalrebel.com

Chapter 18

Living the "YES, AND..." Life

Elizabeth B. Hill, MSW

In my college days, I was immersed in theatre. I lived from one play to another. We did a lot of improv. In improv, we opened ourselves up to the absurd, the ridiculous, to possibility. As we played improv games, we needed to be open to whatever the person presented in the scene and say "Yes, AND!" When your fellow actor told you that you were going to be going to a banana-building factory, if you were to say "eh, I'm not going with you," it would make quite a boring scene. However, if your fellow actor told you that you were going to be going to a banana-building factory, and you said, "YES, I will go with you to the banana-building factory, AND we shall take my boat made out of chocolate ganache and sprinkles!" Oooh, that makes for a far more interesting (and delicious) scene.

As we go about life, we get to decide how we will respond to each possibility we face. Will we say "No," or "Yes" or "Yes, AND"?

Now, there are obviously times that saying, "No" is very important. Saying no and having boundaries can provide a blessed relief and much-needed healing. "No" is a full sentence—no explanation is needed. I've had seasons in my life where letting go, releasing, and saying, "No" were just what were needed at the time. Letting go and saying no allowed me to open up to what was more aligned, and more optimal, for me in the future.

You probably know people, though, that when they hear about a dream or a possibility or goal, they will give you a list of the reasons why that can't be. They seem determined to tell you all the reasons why your dream or your goal is impossible or improbable. They feel driven to tell you all the reasons why your idea won't be able to happen. When faced with their own life, they also have a long list of why they can't have anything other than what they currently have. These people are responded to *possibility* with, "No."

Then there are people who are responding to possibility with, "Yes!" They are open to possibility. They are open to hearing about another's dream. They are open to their dreams. They are encouragers. They want to see people succeed.

Saying "Yes, And..."—whether it be in the context of an improv game, in business, or in any aspect of our lives—takes this one step further. Saying "Yes, and..." is looking for our contribution. When faced with a new possibility that feels in alignment, it means we look for our place within it and the action we could take to further it.

Living our optimal life is about living our life to the fullest, in whatever moment we find ourselves. It is looking at our current situations and the opportunities that present themselves and saying, "Yes, And..." when something feels in alignment. It means seeing the contribution and action we can take towards that possibility.

Living our optimal life doesn't necessarily mean we are living an ideal life or the life of our wildest dreams right now in this moment, although it can lead to that.

It means that we have decided to make the best of our situations, no matter what situation we are faced with, and to be open to possibilities from there.

As my dad says, "We play the cards we're dealt."

Living our optimal life means we look at the cards we were handed and do the best with what we've got.

We don't look at the cards and blame the dealer. We don't blame the cards themselves. We don't declare that we are being *attacked by the universe!* We also don't ignore the cards we have and space out and give up. We look with open eyes at the cards we're dealt, our life in this present moment, and take action from that place.

Living our optimal life can begin at any moment, when we decide to live our life to the fullest with what we have, where we are, and *who* we are, right now.

The beauty of this approach is that if you do this day in and day out, you will find yourself living a life that is beyond anything you could imagine or put on your vision board.

There have been times where I felt I had landed in places that made it very difficult to enjoy the moment. I have thought I have done everything wrong and there was nothing that could be repaired. I have felt trapped, in pain, controlled, out of control, confused, broke, out of options, and ashamed. I have thought I was insane, unworthy of life, and alone.

At some point in my life, I decided to start thinking of life as happening *for* me, rather than *to* me. I began to look for what the situations I found myself in were showing me. In the language of the law of attraction, these experiences were showing me the *contrast* so that I could get clearer on my *desire.*

To live our optimal lives, we tune into what feels truly nurturing and nourishing to our mind, body, and spirit right now.

When we are in touch and in tune with our bodies and souls, we are able to feel when we are in and out of alignment. And our actions may change as a result of this.

As I often share, I feel like I've lived many lives within this lifetime. I've been a wild and free child raised by flower children, a door-knocking minister of Jehovah's Witnesses in my childhood and teens, an artist, a songwriter, an actor, a peace activist, a theatre teacher, a yoga teacher, a social worker, a grant writer, a wife, a mother, a divorced mom, a life coach, a business coach, a behavioral coach, a caregiver to my dear grandma, an author, and a publisher. The work changed, I began and ended relationships, and my purpose has grown and evolved.

A few years ago, when my kids and I into my grandmother's home I knew it was the right choice. I needed to step in and help my mom take care of my grandma. I desired to spend more time with my grandma, who was very dear to me and who I had lived with in my wild college years. I also knew I needed to experience being taken care of for a while. I welcomed a roof over my head and an abundance of food and love in my grandma's home, which I called "the matriarchal palace."

At that moment, moving there was living my optimal life. It was providing for my children the best I knew how to and it was helping my family in a way that I could at the moment. Since I worked from home, I knew I could integrate caring for Grandma while keeping my coaching business at the same time.

After over three years of caregiving, and the COVID-19 pandemic, this stopped being an optimal life. After three years of taking care of Grandma and growing my business (and my children!) at our beloved matriarchal palace, I realized it was time for me and my kids to find our own living space. I had gotten my feet under me after an extremely unhealthy relationship, I had improved my financial situation, and we had gotten precious time with Grandma. Living in the matriarchal palace was a blessing that all of the family had benefited from.

We had also maxed out our ability to be healthy in that environment. Even with having some time away from the house thanks to partnering with my mom, I was still working at least over 100 hours a week being present and caring for my grandma, while caring for my kids and running a coaching business and publishing company, and caring for a house from the 1800s that had been neglected for a long time.

I realized this was completely unsustainable. I looked back and wasn't really sure how I had been doing it. I realized I was barely paying attention to my children. Despite being in the house together a great deal of the time, my attention was always on my grandma or the coaching clients that I met with over Zoom. I realized I only had a few more precious years with my kids before they became officially adults, and I didn't want to miss that in a blink. I also realized that I had been handed a gift from the universe—this blessing beyond my wildest dreams of running a publishing company—and I wanted to proceed with honoring it with the time and focus that it deserved.

So I followed my next desire to live on my own again and focus on my kids and my business. I woke up to the realization that I had worked so hard to raise my kids and grow my business, and I deserved to experience the rewards of that.

While sometimes we may have a clear picture of where we want to go in life, life may have other plans, often even grander than we originally were dreaming of.

I didn't originally set out to start a publishing company. Heck, I didn't even imagine I'd ever be a life coach!

I did, however, always want to be an author and to make the world a better place. The publishing company (and coaching) came to me through my daily actions towards making the world a better place, having one conversation at a time, and being open to possibilities.

Because I took these daily actions led by my desires, the universe has presented me with work beyond anything I ever put on my vision board. First, my desire to teach more yoga classes and workshops led me to become a life coach. This improved my health in all aspects of life: mental, physical, spiritual, and financial. Then from there, I followed my desire to help others by sharing tools that my yoga students and I used to help us decrease our anxiety. This led me to publish my first book. This drew people to me who wanted to do the same. This awakened my desire to help them share their stories in a safe space—and impact the world through our stories. As I began to do this, a light bulb went off in my head (thanks, universe!) and I realized that I could transform Green Heart Living into Green Heart Living Press.

It was only through following my desire and saying "Yes, And!" when people presented opportunities to me, that I was able to find, and live, my optimal life.

Now, I spend my days talking with amazing people who also want to make the world a better place. I get to be creative all day long, talk about people's big dreams, and help them build them. I am very grateful to get to live with my two children and kitty Calypso in Farmington, Connecticut. In just a five-minute walk, I can be on the beautiful grounds of the Hillstead Museum and walk the historic area near Miss Porter's campus. The universe, through the magic of Bumble, has helped me find my sweetheart of a boyfriend, who helps people craft music as I help people craft books. Last year, I was able to attain my goal of hitting the six-figure mark in my business, something I've dreamed of and worked towards for many years. After years of staying close to home, in the past year, I've gotten to travel to Italy, Newport, Block Island, Utah, the Berkshires, and Virginia Beach.

This is my optimal life now. I'm very curious to see where life brings me next. I have my vision boards. I have my strategic plans. I have my bullet journal where I map out all of my goals for each quarter, month, week, and day. (I have given my obsessive nature some healthy tasks to focus on.) And, I know, that if I keep focusing on my alignment in each moment, if I keep approaching each day with a "Yes, And..." mindset, and if I pay attention to opportunities that present themselves, I'll keep living an optimal life that is beyond anything I could have dreamed up for myself.

Integration

- What aspects of your life feel like they are in alignment right now?
- What aspects of your life feel like they are out of alignment right now?
- What is something that you desire right now?
- What is one action you could take today toward that desire?

About Elizabeth

"Living our optimal life can begin at any moment, when we decide to live our life to the fullest with what we have, where we are, and who we are, right now."

Elizabeth B. Hill, MSW, is the CEO and founder of Green Heart Living and Green Heart Living Press. She is the author of *Ignite Your Leadership, Be the Beacon, Embrace Your Space, Success in Any Season, The Great Pause: Blessings and Wisdom from COVID-19, Love Notes: Daily Wisdom for the Soul,* and *Green Your Heart, Green Your World: Avoid Burnout, Save the World and Love Your Life.*

Elizabeth coaches clients through the writing and publishing process to heal, inspire, and grow their impact on the world. Trained as a social worker, yoga teacher, and ontological coach, she weaves creativity, spirituality, and mindfulness into her work with clients. With over 15 years of experience writing for and leading collaborations in the nonprofit sphere, Elizabeth brings a uniquely engaging approach to collaborative book projects. Elizabeth lives in a historic (and hysterical) home in Connecticut with her children and kitty Calypso.

Connect with Elizabeth:
www.GreenHeartLiving.com
Email: liz@greenheartliving.com

Ladies' Power Lunch Resources

Ladies' Power Lunch has so many resources that may be the next step in your LIVING YOUR OPTIMAL LIFE in life and in business.

Free Resources

Connecting with our free resources will be right for you if you are:

- Newer to Ladies' Power Lunch
- If you are newly starting or transitioning your business
- If your business is in the growth phase
- Or if you are looking for outstanding resources to grow your business while managing cash flow

LPL Facebook Group

I invite you to start by going to growsmarternotharder.com /facebook and become a part of our free Ladies Power Lunch community. This community is unlike others in that it is an engaged community of like-minded women in business with only one rule: ***We INTENTIONALLY support each other.***

The theme of our group is: ***You can live your optimal life.*** I truly believe that we can live lives that we drop to our knees in gratitude for each day. A life that is rich and full, fun and joyous, healthy, happy, and passion-filled.

Take advantage of:

- Daily accountability prompts help you grow your business smarter.

- Share about your business and connect with members. Meet networking partners and possible collaboration partners so you can grow with ease and flow.

- Join in for our business growth and personal development sessions. No need to recreate the wheel. There is a member who knows what you need to know and who is willing to share from her heart.

- LPL Book Club. Read motivational and business growth books with other heart-centered friends. Get the main points and identify how these main points can shift your situation for expansive growth in income and impact.

Weekly Networking Opportunities

Hop on in the Zoom room and share about your business, then join the discussion as one of our members shares on a topic of interest to us all. Get to know the women who are here to help you grow.

The LPL TV Show: Grow Your Business Smarter

Live your optimal life. Find us on the Win Win Women Network, your Roku TV, Fire TV, Apple TV or go to growsmarternotharder.com/tv. On the show, we get together the best experts in the field who focus on business growth and personal development and we share their expertise with you, with fun, humor, and authenticity.

The Grow Smarter Handbook

This is your guidebook to getting the most out of this amazing group. My personal tips to making more money and expanding your network using the LPL group. Find it pinned at the top of the LPL Facebook Group.

LPL Podcast

Our podcast expert has taken the best of our business growth/personal development sessions and has made them available to you on our weekly podcast. Find the *Ladies Power Lunch* podcast wherever you get your podcasts!

LPL Blog

Articles to inspire you and help you transform your business. Go to Ladiespowerlunch.com

LPL YouTube

Youtube.ladiespowerlunch.com is where you find a comprehensive archive of even more recordings where our members share their wisdom with us.

Additional Resources

Find more information on these resources at growsmarternotharder.com

LPL Collaborative Collective

Once you have checked out our group a bit, I recommend diving in deeper.

The Collaborative Collective is for the entrepreneur or woman in business who is passionate about what she does and wants to make a difference. She wants to expand her reach and subject matter authority. This is a great opportunity to begin expanding, leveraging, and increasing her impact, reach, and income to the next level.

This resource includes:

- We retreat together: retreats are opportunities for quantum energetic shifts to shortcut your increased income and impact!
- We mastermind together and member match every month! There is no substitute for the power of community when it comes to growth.
- You get to attend the upcoming summit and receive all the summit bonuses.
- You get access to all existing summit replays.
- Access to LPL courses.
- Access to prior summit replays.
- Share your content on the Ladiespowerlunch blog.

LPL Visibility Circle

This is for the entrepreneur or woman in business who is passionate about what she does AND has a story of transformation to share that can truly inspire others. We help these women get their amazing messages out in front of 20-50,000 of their ideal clients using an organized strategy including: public speaking, best-selling collaborative publishing, collaborative marketing, TV, podcasts and so much more.

LPL Amplify

Amplify is for our members who are ready to make a quantum leap into leadership. Benefits at this level are not one size fits all but in general the comprehensive visibility package is not limited to but includes:

1. Personal one-on-one access.
2. Developing your personal visibility strategy.
3. Developing your solo best-selling book project.
4. Developing your solo podcast or TV show.
5. Course development.
6. Developing your signature event or retreat and fitting it seamlessly into your business plan.
7. Essential Quantum Transformational Work.
8. LPL Grow Smarter Butterfly Certification

Let me introduce myself:

By the way, **Hi! I'm Dr. Davia.** I wear a lot of hats, just like you. I'm a mom, a sister, a daughter, and a wife. I help my patients feel better every day. Yet what I'm most passionate about, the thing that gets me out of bed in the morning y'all, is the opportunity to support women in business to live their optimal lives. I do this by helping them to grow their visibility, their reach, their impact, and their income. I'm a beacon for beacons... but it's more than that.

I'm an *amplifier*. I have combined almost two decades of experience in corporate as well as running my own community practice, with my innate ability to translate the energetic signature of the best version of you into words. You know that big dream that you didn't even know you had, for both your business and your life? Step into my field and I can not only translate it but also make it bigger.

I take that higher vision of you and use it to develop a **solid plan for increased visibility**, reach, and success. The result is that you shine your light at its most brilliant. You stop being the world's best-kept secret. Your optimal clients, the ones who are losing sleep at night because they need you, the ones who light up when you work together, are then able to find you with ease and grace, and you can BE THE BEACON that your potential suggests.

My invitation: I'm just going to say it! Will you join our LPL movement? Really and truly and in a heartfelt way? Let us all shine our beautiful lights out into the world. We can do so much more when we do it together.

Selah

About Green Heart Living Press

Green Heart Living Press publishes inspirational books and stories of transformation, making the world a more loving and peaceful place, one book at a time.

Whether you have an idea for an inspirational book and want support through the writing process – or your book is already written and you are looking for a publishing path – Green Heart Living Press can help you get your book out into the world.

You can meet Green Heart authors on the Green Heart Living YouTube channel and the Green Heart Living Podcast.

www.greenheartliving.com

Made in United States
North Haven, CT
12 October 2023

42673236R00111